Llewellyn's
2010
Witches'
Companion

An Almanac for Everyday Living

Llewellyn's 2010 Witches' Companion

ISBN 978-0-7387-0697-9

Cover art © Tim Foley
Cover designer: Gavin Dayton Duffy
Designer: Joanna Willis
Art Director: Lynne Menturweck
Editor: Sharon Leah

Interior illustrations: Rik Olson: 11, 15, 17, 19, 74, 77, 112, 114, 150, 152, 156; Neil Brigham: 23, 27, 28, 31, 134, 138, 196, 201, 202, 205; Tina Fong: 35, 37, 85, 87, 90, 184, 188, 192; Kathleen Edwards: 40, 43, 45, 46, 68, 71, 172, 174, 175, 178, 218, 223, 227; Tim Foley: 9, 51, 53, 55, 62, 65, 81, 82, 119, 159, 161, 166, 181, 242, 245, 247, 249; Lydia Hess: 97, 100, 121, 123, 126, 128, 130, 209, 211, 213; Paul Hoffman: 105, 108, 141, 144, 146, 231, 234, 237

Additional clip art illustrations: Llewellyn Art Department

Any Internet references contained in this work are current at publication time, but the publisher cannot guarantee that a specific location will continue to be maintained.

You can order Llewellyn annuals and books from New Worlds, Llewellyn's magazine catalog. To request a free copy of the catalog, call toll-free 1-877-NEW-WRLD, or visit our Web site at http://subscriptions.llewellyn.com.

Printed in the United States of America.

Llewellyn Worldwide
Dept. 978-0-7387-0697-9
2143 Wooddale Drive
Woodbury, MN 55125-2989
www.llewellyn.com

Contents

Witchy Living • 65

Day-by-Day Witchcraft

Witchcraft Essentials • 119

Practices, Rituals & Spells

Magical Transformations · 181

Everything Old Is New Again

The Lunar Calendar · 253

September 2009 to December 2010

Community Forum

PROVOCATIVE OPINIONS ON
CONTEMPORARY TOPICS

Be Smart About Your Spirituality and Reclaim Your Power

Gail Wood

People turn to religion and spirituality for many reasons. Some long to know there is something special or sacred for them, others long for acceptance and belonging, others seek explanations for the hard questions of life, and still others desire love or power. Whatever our reasons, we can take wrong turns and end up in situations that don't provide what we seek. Instead of finding security, acceptance, and guidance, we may find control, dominance, and disregard.

We saw extreme cases of control, dominance, and disregard for individuals in Waco and Heaven's Gate. When people quote a leader without thinking about or assessing the worth of the message, we are seeing, to a lesser extent, control and dominance. Because religion and spirituality are mysterious and intangible, we often forget to bring our powers of analysis to bear on messages we receive. We tend to accept what our religious

leaders say because we've elevated them to positions of authority and power—we trust them. But when the group or person in power abuses that trust, the betrayal cuts deep and healing is often difficult. Sometimes, when this happens to us, others who are not religious or spiritual may say to the person who has been betrayed, "Get over it." This happens in pagan communities, too. In essence, we place our trust in others because we believe they have more knowledge or experience, and we forget to be smart about our own spirituality.

We're not as trusting when we want to purchase new appliances or vehicles. Most of us do some research. We search the Web, we check standard resources like *Consumer Reports* for neutral comparisons between models, or we ask for references and referrals. In matters of religion and spirituality, however, we often fail to use this analytical skill. We assume too many things about religious people.

When I was younger, I took such a wrong turn and ended up in a Christian cult—a group that can be found on many college campuses. I was young, vulnerable, lost, and longing to be spiritual. So when two evangelists knocked on my door, I was ready and quickly inculcated into the group. I allowed them to have power over my money, to choose my friends, and to determine my sexuality. Over and over

I allowed someone else to think for me, even when my gut instinct told me something was wrong. The group mind was more powerful than my own mind. Not having the power or experience to overtly defy the allure of the group, I questioned through joking and self-sabotage. I went from being a golden girl to feeling like a failure. After the group dropped me, members and former friends shunned me. I was left alone.

I rebuilt my life and spent time trying to understand why that had happened. People were quick to tell me that it would never happen to them because they were too smart. Some suggested that it was because I was weak that those events had happened to me. Perhaps that was true. Certainly, the criticism hurt me to my core for quite some time. Eventually, I forgave myself for being young, open-hearted, trusting, vulnerable, and accepting what others said without doing enough thinking. It wasn't smart of me to surrender my own power to someone because they seemed to know more or to be more powerful or experienced.

It wasn't easy, but I learned to be smart about my spirituality. I had to spend time examining my failure. I had to gather the internal strength to look at what happened and learn from it so I could come to an understanding of myself and the role spirituality has in my life—to be a strong, powerful, thinking adult. At first my motivation to do all the hard work grew out of my determination to not make the same mistake again. Then, later, I did the work so I could find the spiritual home for which I still longed.

In those days, there wasn't a lot of talk about spiritual abuse, but there was a great deal of awareness about domestic violence and abuse. Some of the literature on emotional abuse was very helpful. I read about dominance, intimidation, and isolation, as well as control over money, children, and sex. Eventually, I found Isaac Bonewits' book *Real Magic*, which contains his "Cult Evaluation Danger" framework. (With Bonewit's permission, the information is also available from *Wicca Coven* by Judy Harrow on the Internet). From those sources, I developed good questions to ask myself when thinking about spiritual groups and spiritual teachers. The questions fell into some general categories:

Group Behavior and Group Mind

- Does the group promote compliance and/or dependence?

- Does the group or leader employ language or actions that make me feel small or insignificant?

- Does the group allow (or punish) questioning, satire, and/or dissent?

- How does the group handle money issues?

- How does the group treat the leader's strengths and weaknesses?

- How does the group handle leaving the group, and how are the people treated afterwards?

- How does the group honor individual strengths and weaknesses?

- Is the group joyful even in times of adversity?

- Is there kindness, compassion, mercy, forgiveness, humor, and a healthy outlook on others outside the group and on life?

Group Relationship to External Influences

- Does the group promote an "us" versus "outsider" mentality?

- How does the group encourage or discourage relationships with other groups or individuals?

- Does the group require adherence to particular political or social views?

Group Leader Behavior

- Does the leader have a sense of humor?

- Are the leader's views clear, consistent, and transparent?

- How does the leader treat his/her own weaknesses and strengths?

- Is the leader supportive (not belittling) of everyone?

- Does the group allow for mistakes, and is it respectful of human fallibility, including the fallibility of the leaders?

- How is the leader treated by members of the group?

- How does the leader handle change, dissent, disagreement, accolades, and mistakes?

Group Treatment of Individuals

- Does the group allow you to set your own priorities for home, work, and family?

- Are you able to make your own decisions about your life, or are you compelled to follow the rules of the group even when they conflict with your own values?

For several years afterwards, I did presentations on cults on campuses where I worked. I went into residence halls and taught student populations, faculty, staff, and sometimes the parents how to protect themselves from becoming entangled in cult behavior. One thing I emphasized was that, on some level, the individual does decide to give up his or her power and to allow a group to make decisions for them. We all need to look at that situation without blaming the individual; it is something that happens because we are young, vulnerable, and poorly trained in spiritual matters and spiritual group behavior.

One of the things I had to endure during those presentations was people who said they would never get involved in a cult because they weren't as "weak," "stupid," "naïve," or "gullible" as I was. I would respond without arguing against their judgment of me because I had learned that my own inner strength, will, and courage were enough. Those presentations were a rite of passage. I learned to gather my courage and will and to speak my own truth, and I knew I had learned those lessons well when a student asked me: "If you could go back and change your decision, would you decide not to do it?" I replied that those five years and the subsequent understanding I gained had profoundly changed me and that I was happy with who I had become. It was a difficult question to answer because it wasn't the five years in a cult that changed me, it was the work I had done on the spiritual, emotional, and psychological levels that led me to become who I am. I am a strong, confident, courageous spirited woman. I survived not only a cult but also grief, sorrow, death, and despair, and I am still able to embrace joy, delight, pleasure, and happiness. Interestingly, the requests for those presentations stopped shortly after that session. The lessons were learned: I have claimed my power, and I stand in it.

Power is a word that carries a lot of negative connotations. In the past twenty years, Starhawk and the Reclaiming Collective's teachings have redefined power as dominance, shared power, and empowerment. Their work has helped pagans and others to understand the nature of power and its uses. Nevertheless, many people think power is the tool that dictators, bosses, politicians, and other leaders use for their own purposes and designs. Generally, we don't think of power as something we share with others or use for the greater good. Shamans and shamanic practitioners know that power is a good thing, something to be gained and used for the highest good in service to community, the gods, and self. It is how and why we use power that is important to understand.

Where does personal power come from? It comes from our own core knowledge of ourselves, our own personal authority. If we have a clear, strong, honest understanding of our abilities, then we are able to harness our power and use it effectively, while striving to act from a place of compassion and integrity. If we are less than honest about our own abilities, our actions and power may be tainted by our weaknesses. Our authority becomes arrogant and dominating, which causes us to become defensive or manipulative.

Standing in our power, finding our inner authority, and speaking our truths are learned behaviors that become skills with consistent understanding and practice. As with physical exercise, we can strengthen our core when we exercise those inner muscles. When we do this on an emotional and spiritual level, our spiritual muscles become stronger, more flexible, and more able to help us make good decisions about our lives. Each time we exercise personal will and make decisions for our own highest good, we become stronger and more courageous. When we begin to understand our own personal spirituality and assume responsibility for it, we become powerful.

To know yourself is to connect with your inner divinity and work from that experience and understanding. To know that all of you—mind, body, and soul—is special and sacred is essential knowledge

as you walk in a world that doesn't always honor people as spiritual beings, regardless of their religion or spiritual path.

It is sometimes hard for us to hear our inner divinity because our inner critic is so strong and so loud. The inner critic is that voice that causes us to question every decision, worry about every detail, and compare ourselves to other people. If you are unable to keep the inner critic in perspective, that critic can become a saboteur in your life, leaving you with constant worry and without joy, never able to forgive or forget. The critic is not the voice of the Goddess within us—the divine spark that holds us beloved. Your inner sacred voice will hold your responsible but, at the same time, it will also provide you with peace and compassion.

The first step in strengthening your personal authority is to harness the power of your inner critic and lead it to be more positive and nurturing. You need to understand your inner critic and recognize its voice. An inner critic will create rules and set impossibly high standards and then blame or berate you when things violate those rules. Your inner critic is the one who makes you stand at the mirror and call yourself names, such as stupid, ugly, weak, or incompetent. Your inner critic will compare you to others and find you lacking; it will catalog every failure and every shortcoming. Your inner critic will exaggerate your failures and weaknesses, saying you are "always" a failure. Your inner critic is constantly on the attack and never nurturing. One of the exercises you can do when the messages start is to tell your inner critic to stop or to shut up (in as loud a voice as is necessary).

On the other hand, your inner sacred voice is always supporting you and coaching you. If you fail, your inner sacred will comfort you and help you discover ways to succeed. Your inner sacred voice is warm, kind, and helpful. The first step is to believe the inner voice. So rather than stand at the mirror and proclaim your ugliness, stand at the mirror and honor something beautiful about yourself. As you continue to do this and begin to smile, you will find a new light shining from you. More things will become acceptable and then beautiful. Your inner sacred voice will always give you positive words about your essential self. Your inner sacred is love and you are love. It will take some time for you to absorb that knowledge into your conscious and unconscious mind, but it is worth the effort.

Your inner sacred voice will hold you accountable. The voice is warm, nurturing, and kind, but it is a voice of truth delivered with compassion and mercy. That's why this spiritual path is not for sissies. We cannot retreat into negativity but, instead, stand strong and

face our flaws and correct them. When you do make mistakes, your inner sacred voice will point that out without blame or harsh criticism. Listening to this voice takes courage and when you do listen, your inner core strength will grow. As you act on the positive nature of your inner sacred, you will find that you are more confident, more sure of your own authority. You can articulate your needs and beliefs and feel good about yourself.

When your inner critic is under control and your inner sacred voice is strong, you will find a new enthusiasm about life. Even when the circumstances of your outer life are far from ideal, you will find that your interior is strong and joyful, and you will be enthusiastic and hopeful about change. Enthusiasm has its roots in the Latin word for "the god within," and you will find that you are better able to pursue your goals, make change, and create a life that fits your ideals and desires.

One of the rules I have for myself is: If it isn't fun, don't do it. What I mean is that when the going gets tough and you can't find that inner place of joy, then it's time to make changes. You will not be exempt from grief, sorrow, mistakes, or pain. You will be able to deal with them from a place of power, authority, love, and strength, however. The beauty, power, and authority of your inner core will shine out into the world, and the positive and glorious things you seek in life will find their way to you. Others will think you are lucky, and you will know that your luck comes from the work of a strong inner core and a wonderful, loving sacred voice. You will sing the songs of the sacred because you hear them every minute from within.

In the pagan community, I often run into people who have been in a group that left them feeling damaged or rejected. Many of these pagans decide to become solitaries because they believe there is no such thing as a good group and often voice anti-coven or anti-group rhetoric. The truth is that within the pagan community there are a multiplicity of experiences that are as varied as the pagan community itself. There are bad groups, and there are groups that are bad for you but good for others. And just as being solitary is good for many people, it is not so good for others. But people who decide to be solitaries because "all groups are bad" are doing themselves a disservice.

An alternative action is to take an unflinching look at the situation and assess how your own behavior may or may not have contributed to these experiences. It's very difficult because you must resist blaming yourself and feeling ashamed. It takes courage and willpower to take a good strong look in the mirror of our actions, to resist blame and get to the truths, whether they are pleasant or unpleasant. You will be more powerful for taking this action. It is part of the expectation of the witch and pagan that extends as far back as ancient Greece to a time when the Delphic Oracle instructed seekers to "know thyself." After taking an honest, compassionate view of the circumstances, including your reaction to it and the outcome, you can know that your decision to be in a group or to be a solitary was made from that core center of strength and power. You can stand in your power and take responsibility for your spiritual actions because you know yourself.

Gail Wood *started her writing career when a story she wrote in the first grade was posted on the board by her teacher. The story was about Jo-Jo the monkey. Her mother saved that story for Gail. She is the author of* Rituals of the Dark Moon: 13 Rites for a Magical Path *published by Llewellyn in 2001. Currently, she lives in a 100+ year-old house with her partner Mike and their two dogs. Mike shares her spiritual interests and is an exceptionally fine priest, who is following the ecstatic path of Gaia.*

Illustrations: Rik Olson

Giving Back to the Spirit World

Lupa

Many pagans believe in animism and attribute a spirit to plants, animals, and even inanimate objects. The reasons why someone chooses to work with specific spirits and how they work with the spirits vary from individual to individual. Too often, however, pagans only engage with these spirits in abstract terms and only when they are in the circle or other ritual space. But just because someone claims to have a nature-based belief system does not mean that communication occurs between them and nature or that the spirit of the plant, animal, or rock, is taken into consideration. To many

of us it would seem appropriate to hold a ritual for a water spirit or water nymph near a particular (often convenient) body of water. Frequently, though, people don't check to see whether the specific nymph being worked with is fond of that particular waterway, or not. This distance between our abstract perceptions of what is appropriate and what is reality can cause a certain amount of dissonance.

A good example of dissonance between perception and reality can be found among our conservation and environmental stewardship practices. Quite a number of pagans claim to have totem animals. Yet, some of these same folks give little attention to the environments in which the physical counterparts of their totems live. If you have Frog as a totem and given that frogs are among the most pollution-sensitive creatures out there, it would make sense to give honor to Frog by promoting a lifestyle that takes pollution into consideration. But as we have detached ourselves from an engaged relationship with the natural world, so have we detached our perceptions from the reality of the entities we work with in our spiritual practices. This happens with totems and other spirits, as well as with deities and other beings.

To be fair, for some pagans, paganism isn't about nature worship. It's about honoring the gods and spirits in a manner that is culturally appropriate or an approximation of what some ancient civilization practiced. For others, paganism is, in a general sense, more about fertility. And, of course, those pagans with "magpie syndrome" are easily distracted by shiny objects. However, I would like to ask you, the reader, to take the natural world into consideration in your spirituality.

We each have different directions in which to focus our paths, including some mentioned in the previous paragraph, but why only study one possibility to the exclusion of all others? We can consider nature, give honor to those spirit beings that share our lives with us, and promote the health and fertility of living beings all at once. We can even keep the "magpies" happy while we're at it!

Making Connections

The first step in this process is to make connections between the "spirits" (and deities, etc.—but I'll just use "spirits" for short) you work with and the natural phenomena they embody or are otherwise associated with.[1] This may be relatively easy to do with some spirits, such as animal, plant, and mineral totems. For others, like animal-headed Egyptian deities, where the connection is a bit more

---

1. Granted, there are spirits that embody abstract human concepts, such as justice or peace. In this case, you may seek out natural phenomena that are associated with these concepts if there are none in the traditional lore.

abstract, making the connection between the deities and the animals whose heads they bear may be tougher.

You may argue that ancient cultures only nominally and symbolically connected a particular animal with a deity and that those ancient people didn't actually believe that a deity was an animal. That may be true. However, there's something to be said for flexibility. We are not living in an ancient world. We are in the twenty-first century, and we cannot escape that fact no matter how many cultural reconstructions, Ren fairs, or historical fictions we may encounter. And people in twenty-first century industrialized nations are facing very different problems than our ancestors did.

> ... spirits don't have to be nature spirits. Have you ever tried talking to the spirit of a building or other man-made place?

Try going deeper than just the *semiotics* (study of signs and symbols and their use in interpretation). If you worship a sky deity, for example, observe a thunderstorm or the passing of clouds. Now, think of air pollution and about sticking your head near an exhaust pipe and taking a *deep* breath (but don't actually do it!). Is that a fit offering for a deity whose domain is supposed to be the actual, physical sky above or, for that matter, who may be embodied in that sky?

Regardless of where you focus your relationships with spirits, try getting in touch with the physical, natural phenomena that are associated with them. Even in an urban area you can find earth, air, fire, and water.[2] If you want to be really precise, ask each spirit to show you to their preferred place. Explore the qualities of the phenomena. Where,

---

2. *City Magick* (Weiser, 2001) by Christopher Penczak and *The Urban Primitive* (Llewellyn, 2002) by Raven Kaldera and Tannin Schwartzstein are two good books on making these connections in urban areas.

as an example, might the behavior of physical squirrels relate to the nature of Ratatosk, the squirrel in Norse mythology that scurries up and down Yggdrasil (the world tree)? If you have access to an ocean, consider the awe-struck reaction many people must have had to such a huge body of water (as well as its potential danger) and how their reactions may have contributed to myths about sea deities.

We can also ask the spirits themselves about their relationships with various phenomena. The totems I work with have generally appreciated offerings in the form of volunteerism and donations to nonprofit groups that work to protect wildlife and habitats, as well as my attempts to live a greener lifestyle. These offerings aid the spirit's physical "children."

If you have ideas for ways to honor a spirit through physical phe-nomena, ask the spirit if it would be acceptable. You don't have to give up more historically accurate practices. Simply integrate solutions for twenty-first-century problems into your path in nonconflicting ways.

Local Spirits

Another overlooked practice is that of connecting with the spirits in your own back yard, so to speak. Many pagans focus so heavily on spirits from other cultures that they don't even think about the local spirits. Yet, when we interact with physical reality, whether in rural or urban settings, some of the greatest lessons and influences come to us from those spirits. After all, we're on their home turf!

For most of my totemic practice, I worked with the totems of animals I'd never seen in person outside of a zoo or sanctuary. Wolf came to me when I was very young. Later on I worked with Bear, Badger, even Silver Dollar (yes, the fish found in aquariums, as well as the Amazon River). However, it wasn't until I moved to Portland, Oregon, in 2007, that I really began connecting with the *genius loci* (spirits of the land) in more than a vague sort of way. I got to know

Scrub Jay, Fox Squirrel, Crow, and Banana Slug. They could demonstrate things about their home that non-native spirits were much less familiar with.

Again, spirits don't have to be nature spirits. Have you ever tried talking to the spirit of a building or other man-made place? Cities and the individual spirits within them are open to communication just as much as are the spirits of trees, gardens, and urban wildlife.

Take some time to talk to the spirits in your area. Start at home, and work your way slowly outward. If this takes a while, don't fret; there's no time limit on this. You may find, over time, that these spirits can help you with specific things. If you're looking for a job so you can stay in a particular place, ask the spirit of that place for assistance in your job hunt. If that place really likes you, it may put in a good bit of effort to keep you around. Having a good relationship with the spirits around you can make being in your environment much more pleasant. You'll also have a better knowledge about individual features—where you are most welcome and where you may want to avoid. You can even ask the local spirits if there are things they might ask you to do to improve the environment you share.

Those We Depend On

Since there are a number of pagan religious paths that deal with fertility, including that of the plants and animals, there are numerous overarching spirits and deities associated with ensuring continued fertility. Again, though, these are often somewhat more abstract in their connections to the process of fertility.

Every day we depend on numerous other beings for our very survival. There are many areas in which this is true; however, for the sake of brevity, I'm going to focus on one of the most important: food. Everyone needs to eat, and no amount of technology and industrialization is going to completely divorce us from the natural cycles required to feed us. As with so many areas of our lives, there are plenty of specific spirits who are often overshadowed by the overarching, "bigger" ones, such as deities.

I work extensively with a group of totems that I call "food totems." In my experience, all animals (and plants) have totems. Totems are archetypal beings that embody all the qualities of a given species, though unlike Jung's concept of archetypes, they aren't just in our

heads. Food totems are the totems of species that are most commonly associated with food. In the United States this includes Cow, Chicken, Crab, Pig, Duck, Salmon, and others.

Many of these animals, particularly the domesticated ones, aren't given much regard at all. I'm sure you've heard pigs referred to as "smelly" and cows and chickens as "stupid." And that's about the extent of most people's opinions of these beings. However, I've worked with Chicken, Pig, and others. They are not limited to the negative stereotypes applied to their physical counterparts. I have no doubt that this also ties in with the absolutely appalling manner in which most animals bred for food in the United States are raised and killed. When people have no respect for a being, the treatment of the animal reflects that. People would get angry about the death of a well-regarded animal, such as a dog, but care little about a chicken.

Before I go further, I want to emphasize that for reasons that include my health, I am an omnivore. That I eat meat in addition to fruits, vegetables, and grains is even more reason for me to work with animal-food totems. However, as an animist, I also believe that plants have spirits and that while they may not have nervous systems, those spirits also suffer from ill treatment. If you are vegetarian, vegan, or even omnivorous, try applying the concept of food totems to plants, as well.

One of the things I try to do, when I can afford to, is buy free-range, organic meat and eggs. Eventually, I would like to raise my own small livestock for food so I will know exactly where my food comes from. While I realize that animals still have to die to provide meat, if their lives and deaths were better than factory farming "standards," it's at least somewhat of an improvement.

Sometimes, when preparing meat, I will do full rituals as a way to honor the spirit of the animal that wore the flesh, as well as the corresponding totem. Other times, I simply talk to the spirits and totems during meals to let them know I am aware of them.

The next time you eat something, stop for a moment and consider what beings contributed to your meal. Did a plant or animal die? Were pesticides used to kill insects? Were rats and mice trapped in the processing plants? Did the farmer shoot foxes or other predators to prevent loss of livestock? Were deer and other herbivores killed to protect crops? These are a few of the beings that were potentially impacted—and that's not even considering the people who are involved, or the pollution that is created.

Our entire lives are composed of interconnections. Sadly, too many people perceive themselves as isolated beings who have with little impact on the world. Yet every decision we make has an effect on others, including spirits of various sorts. Even if those spirits are currently in physical bodies, are they not worth our regard?

Learning to Give Back

I mentioned a few things about aiding and honoring spirits associated with food, but what about other spirits? Here are a few more ideas for real-world efforts that make wonderful offerings for the spirits around us.

Earth-friendly Offerings

Pagans often leave offerings outdoors for the various spirits they work with. Unfortunately, some of these offerings, while they may be well intended, aren't so great for the environment. Leaving a food offering, especially if a ritual contained cakes and ale or similar things, is often done with the intent that local animals will be fed. Many of the things we eat, though, aren't at all good for other animals (and in some cases, aren't good for us, either!). Bread, for example, is pretty devoid of nutrition compared to what most wild animals eat. You can literally starve ducks to death by feeding them bread. They fill up on the bread and then don't feel motivated to eat their natural foods, which have the nutrients they actually need.

Additionally, when wild animals learn to associate food with humans, things generally go badly for the animals. Besides the greater potential of being hit by cars or injured or killed by people or domestic pets, these animals may have their instincts dampened over time. There are already numerous cases in the United States of Canada geese that don't migrate any more. And coyotes and bears in Yellowstone National Park will assault vehicles in search of food rather than maintain their natural foraging habits. This doesn't mean you have no options for offerings. Nonprofits that work to preserve wildlife habitats or other natural phenomena that may be sacred to the spirits you work with will appreciate donations. If you're an artist, you could hold a sale or auction to raise money. And, while domestic animals aren't quite as "natural" as wolves and bobcats, your local animal shelters are always happy to accept donations of quality pet food.

Activist Magic

In my experience, spirits tend to be quite cooperative when you're working magic for their benefit or the benefit of people, animals, plants, and so forth, which they hold dear. This can be as simple as a spell or an elaborately planned group ritual with all the works. Pay attention to current events, particularly proposed legislation and other events that could significantly affect whatever cause for which you and the spirits are working magic. Sending letters to your elected officials to let them know your thoughts on various issues is always a good choice, and it doesn't take up much time.

One word of advice: when working with activist magic, be as specific as possible in your focus. I've been to a number of rituals that were designed to "wrap the world in white light" or some similar sentiment. However, think of activist magic as shooting at a target. If you use a shotgun, you'll hit the tar-

get—and everything around it. If you use a rifle and aim more carefully, one bullet can hit the target dead center. Activist magic is the same way; you'll get better results if you carefully plan to affect only one issue or factor, than if you did something more general that spreads your efforts too thin.

Conclusion

While I've focused primarily on issues of conservation and environmentalism, you can take the concepts I've discussed in other directions. If your patron deity protects women, give donations to a women's shelter. Or if you work with spirits who are fond of liberty and freedom, give some time to promote and preserve civil rights—and set an example by the way you choose to live. Look at the virtues the spirits promote or embody, and integrate those virtues into your life.

Your political stances may be different than mine, and the same goes for the worldview of the spirits you work with. While there's a time and place to be in "a world between worlds," to work with abstract rituals and symbolic archetypes, there are also times to connect the spiritual and the physical in more concrete ways. Contrary to popular belief, spiritual and physical are not a dichotomy. If we truly believe in something, it behooves us to support those beliefs not only in our litanies and rituals, but in the mundane life we live on a daily basis.

Lupa *is a pagan and experimental magician living in Portland, Oregon, with her husband and fellow author, Taylor Ellwood. She is the author of* Fang and Fur, Blood and Bone: A Primal Guide to Animal Magic, A Field Guide to Otherkin, *and* Kink Magic: Sex Magic Beyond Vanilla *(cowritten with Taylor and published in Stafford, UK: Immanion Press). She may be found online at http://www.thegreenwolf.com.*

Illustrations: Neil Brigham

Creating a Safe Environment at Pagan Gatherings

Ann Moura

The face of paganism is changing dramatically. The media is paying attention to pagan events and gatherings, and we need to acknowledge this reality and make the adjustments that will allow paganism to evolve in harmony with the rest of society. Pagan outreach to the general public is currently being accomplished on many levels to educate society about the spiritual paths of pagans as genuine religions under legal protection of the law. But we have a dichotomy. On the one hand, we try to eradicate the negative image of pagans as evil threats to society or civil order. On the other hand, we are unsure about how much we are willing to conform to society in order to participate in the benefits and respect granted to bona fide religions.

On the positive side, the Supreme Court has recognized Wicca as a religion, the pentacle has been granted for the memorials of deceased military pagans, and pagans are represented at worldwide religious councils, prison chaplain corps, military service, business, and community work. On the negative side, we still have people in high offices saying that Wicca is not a real religion and that pagans are evil, unethical, and immoral.

It is time to decide on which side of the fence we belong. How can we blend the pagan tradition of freedom and uninhibited spirituality with the laws and restrictions of society? It is not uncommon to see alcohol consumption and nudity at pagan gatherings and events held in counties or in public and national parks, where alcohol or nudity are illegal. Often, at these events, small children run around the site naked and unattended by their parents, and teenage girls roughhouse topless or in sheer clothing with teenage boys while unrelated adults watch. And nude adults dance in front of youngsters, and vice versa, at drum circles. And illegal drugs are often used.

Fortunately, we have not been faced with a national press about a gathering gone wrong. But it is time to reassess whether or not we are inadvertently exposing our children to criminal charges or, worse, to predators. As paganism grows, though, so does the attention being paid to us. And we need to pay attention, in turn, to news events about other unconventional groups that involve well-meaning people who have manipulated the law. The media has exposed them in the name of child welfare and protecting society. A chance encounter by nonpagan people at an event, a clandestine photo of a nude youngster posted on the Internet, or a mishap caused by drinking or drug use at a gathering could bring everyone at the

event under public scrutiny and fuel the fires of righteous indignation against pagans.

Paganism has emerged into the mainstream. Gatherings are mellowing into family-oriented spiritual retreats with day care and crafts for children, cultural-heritage exploration, workshops for youth and adult groups, ministerial training, rites of passage, and public rituals. It is wonderful to see the next generation coming into their own, but we need to have a worthy heritage for them to assume and carry on. We need to provide them with the tools to comprehend the difference between acceptable nudity and potential threats to their well-being. We must patrol our gatherings to keep child molesters, sexual predators, rapists, and drug dealers from using pagan events to seek out potential victims. We must also guide our young people on how to tread the path between what is appropriate behavior at gatherings and what might not be acceptable to their non-pagan peers. Impressionable children and young people, for their own emotional and mental well-being, need to be protected from harassment and persecution in school and in their neighborhoods.

We need to protect our children from social confusion and the condemnation of their non-pagan peers who equate paganism with loose morals, promiscuity, and evil. We need to protect attendees of all ages from being at risk due to the actions of others. It is time to acknowledge that greater self-regulation is needed at pagan events and gatherings. It should be apparent that unregulated or poorly regulated events are flirtations with disaster. The time for addressing how to balance an alternative lifestyle and religious freedom with the desire for public recognition of paganism as spiritually legitimate is now.

Things are changing. For example, vending has grown from being a cottage industry to being a full-scale industry. And vendors are expected to have business licenses, collect taxes, and keep records of sales. Authorities have grounds to check for these things—even on private property—and to hold vendors accountable or shut them down.

Should authorities and code-enforcement arrive at a gathering, what else might attract their attention? Nudity? Illegal drinking or drug use? When nudity is part of the event, we need to ensure that it is healthy and not provocative. If events need permits, these must be acquired and followed. The responsibility is huge, and event organizers and Guardians must be trained and prepared to deal with inappropriate behavior—no matter who is involved. Most event participants are unaware of the tensions, disputes, upsets, complaints, and abuse situations generally handled quietly and efficiently by organizers. Counseling, reprimanding, and expelling offenders usually goes unnoticed by others. The danger lies in an incident getting out of control to where the police are called in. Subsequent investigations could have a deleterious affect on those who prefer privacy and whose lives are suddenly open to public debate or condemnation.

A well-trained, recognizable, and insured Guardian corps that consists of people who are mentally and physically equipped to handle problems and emergencies is essential to a gathering. Most

Guardians are amazing and inspire a sense of security and confidence, but some lack training, focus, or discernment to know what constitutes aberrant behavior and a situation that is becoming dangerous, or how to react to or resolve a matter.

Families attend gatherings to interact with other families and a greater pagan community not available in their home area. Normally, these events are a wonderful experience for children and young teens, but the more family-oriented pagan events become, the more discretion is needed in determining what constitutes appropriate behavior. If paganism is to have the respect and recognition accorded to other religions and spiritualities, it must guard against, and disassociate from, what society and the law in general consider unhealthy elements and dangerous behavior.

There are some excellent gatherings where people feel safe and secure, where Guardians are dependable and well-instructed, where the organizers take immediate action when there is trouble without disturbing the other attendees, but it needs to go further. A spiritual path must not endanger its participants. Guardians and organizers must address the issues and not ignore them.

It falls to parents, organizers, and attendees to be on their guard against people and situations that could harm our children or besmirch the reputation of pagans everywhere. As a community, pagans need to draw some lines and be willing to back them up with action. To do otherwise is to ignore reality and to endanger those who approach paganism as seekers and perhaps unwittingly expose themselves to abuse. It is time for pagans to consider the larger consequences for everyone should something go wrong at a gathering. Organizers need to create guidelines to keep the event legal, publish the guidelines, hand them out to all who enter the grounds, and enforce them. For the good of all, let none—especially our next generation—be harmed by the addictions or predilections of another.

Ann Moura *holds both a Bachelor of Arts and Master of Arts degree in history and writes from personal experience and family training. Her books currently available through Llewellyn Worldwide and in many bookstores include:* Green Witchcraft: Folk Magic; Fairy Lore, & Herb Craft; Green Witchcraft II: Balancing Light & Shadow; Green Witchcraft III: The Manual; Green Magic: The Sacred Connection to Nature; Grimoire for the Green Witch: A Complete Book of Shadows; *and* Tarot for the Green Witch. *She can be contacted through her Web site at http://www.annmourasgarden.com.*

Illustrations: Tina Fong

Where are the Pagan Communities?

Boudica

Paganism has a unique spiritual path in that we decide for ourselves our personal ethical standards, and we set our own values of morality. While there is a rede that is from the Wiccan traditions, it is not a law. It is advice—a council—and whether you adapt that rede is up to you. We have embraced the pagan culture because we believe in the concept of free will, and this belief carries over into our pagan spirituality. We feel we are intelligent enough to make our own decisions about spirituality and the associated philosophies. We choose the paths we walk, be they

sexual, environmental, social, magical, or spiritual. We are not dictated to, we are not told what to believe, what social structure we have to adhere to, or what magical practice we need to follow. No one speaks for us. There are no set leaders representing the "whole" pagan community.

One drawback of the pagan path, though, is the gross lack of genuine community among pagans. We acknowledge our groups and we work together—when our egos do not get in the way, when it is convenient for us to do it, or when it costs us little or nothing to participate. I have found, at times, that pagans are more willing to spend a dollar than put in time for a cause. We find excuses for not being part of a group, or we give convoluted reasons for why we feel that "this or that" does not apply to "me." While this is not indicative of all pagans, we have five million pagans in the United States and the number is said to be growing annually, so why do we not see these numbers represented in our communities?

I recognize that our independence of thought has led to responsible community growth with real environmental advances as well as real community growth and improvement to the quality of life of the pagans involved in these projects. But I suggest that for many pagans, the path has led to isolation. Why and how do we need to be more responsible to our own membership? Why include those who stand on the fringe of the circle looking in?

We need to open our doors and our hearts to all pagans out there who feel they don't have to be part of anything because in times of need, what we could really use is the support, friendship, and love of fellow pagans who share common values and cherish the same freedoms. I present here an essay for your consideration. I judge no one, as we all have our own concepts and values.

. . . .

The word *solitary* has come to mean a lot of different things within the pagan community. Many times, sadly, it is taken as meaning "alone." Some people use it as an excuse to separate themselves from any community. But a most basic human need is for a social environment—to belong. Studies found on the Web show that a lack of a social environment is a breeding ground for many social "diseases." Lack of a social environment has been labeled a breeding ground for depression and associated mental health issues. A quick search on www.Google.com of "social environment and health" will uncover discussions on how a lack of social environment can lead to inequities in service. One example of inequity in service is that many people do not know about, and therefore are not able to access, better healthcare choices. That is just one issue out of many.

We see some of this in our own communities. We see many pagans only when they are in need, which may lead us to think we are a very needy group. But the truth is, we "need" no more and no less than anyone else. We come to realize that while we may want to be independent, we also cannot exist alone.

So how can we, as pagans, fit into a social structure and still maintain our independence? How can we establish communities where we can work together as a group without compromising our individuality and diversity? We are just as responsible for inaction as we are for our action. For all that we feel we do, if we ignore what needs to be done and leave "whatever" up to someone else to take care of, are we not trying to limit our responsibility, and in doing so, are we not also limiting our personal freedoms?

When it comes to *me*, what affects *me* should also affect the entire pagan community. We scream about it when it happens to "me," and we get indignant when it affects "us." Otherwise, it is someone else's responsibility. How does this fit into the concept of being "responsible"? I would like to point out that the whole earth exists not only to be our responsibility but to be our home. It's where we learn to live together, to work together, and to enable each other just as we enable ourselves.

Freedom and Responsibility

Because we make these choices for ourselves, we are also responsible for the actions we take. We live by these choices and acknowledge that no one else made them for us. We take responsibility for making sure our actions are courteous of others and within the confines of social laws. If we make a poor choice, we admit that it was our own action. We can do nothing else because we have acknowledged freedom of choice—free will—and we have exercised those rights.

When we err, we acknowledge the error, make restitution if necessary, learn from the lesson, and move on. If we choose to ignore the law and get arrested or fined, we are responsible for acknowledging we broke a law, paying the restitution, and then furthering the action by seeking to  prove the law has no practical value to the community and that it is the product of an outdated law or bias reasoning. If we fail to show cause, we must accept the public stance and adhere to the rules that society feels it needs to establish a proper atmosphere for its membership. We have no recourse at that point, other than to know we did our best and to accept that we don't always win.

We also choose to be independent of the rules of organizations when it comes to spirituality. We usually do not belong to large organizations or denominations, though we may congregate from time to time with larger groups. There are exceptions, but, realize that these so-called "larger organizations" in no way rival the size of well-established religious congregations. For the most part, these are independent groups that form their own social structures. These social structures may interact with other social structures from time to time, but they will remain independent. Even smaller than this are the groups of solitary practitioners and then the individual practitioners themselves. The choice to be independent thinkers can sometimes lead us to believe that we can be independent of each other.

The individuals who run these organizations do not represent the pagan community at large. They speak mostly for themselves and the organization they represent, and the membership chooses to follow that organization as long as it continues to represent the individual's needs. This is the nature of the beast, and it is why many organizations within the pagan community fail. If the focus changes just a little, it may not mesh with the original members' thoughts on the organization, and those members move on to find other organizations, or not, that will meet their needs.

When we take steps to be independent and self-governing, we must also realize that we take on the responsibility to work within accepted social structures and to do so without compromising our independence. It is a difficult situation to balance, and we do encounter conflict. Laws may not permit our freedom to, say, dress or undress as we would like in areas that may be deemed public. Our responsibility is to know this and to be aware of where we can exercise our rights. Or if we feel that this law is biased in some manner, it is our responsibility to pursue legal action to have it examined for purpose and removed if it is indeed not for the better of the whole.

When we encounter conflict, we need to understand that ignorance is not an excuse. While we have been taught for a couple of thousand years that we are not "ultimately responsible" for our actions because of a spiritual force or that "environmental" issue, as pagans we accept the notion of independence of ideas and freedom of thoughts. We accept the ability to do away with the spiritual force that supposedly "made us do it" or the restraints of being labeled a "product of our environment." We deny the concept of enforced restriction as much as we accept the concept of free will. These restrictions are challenges that we need to see and overcome in order to be freethinkers and independent spirits. If we do not, we remain captives of a system that will control and manipulate our lives. We need to deny the conventional concepts of restriction in order to achieve the standards we set for ourselves. As you can see, what we perceive as freedom can be just as restricting as that which we perceive to be the cause for why we are not free.

We have tools at our disposal to deny the conventional concepts. We have laws to assure our freedoms, and we can enforce those laws by exercising our rights to challenge any decisions that restrict our rights. We have attained the recognition we have today by protesting and by challenging the status quo.

From pagan headstones to recognition of our status as nonprofit and charitable organizations that exist without the usual defined concepts of organization, we have created change. That we are able to perform legal marriages in some states without the process of ordination or the association with an "officially recognized" religious group is a direct result of challenging the system. We have gotten really good at challenging.

But in our quest to challenge, we find that we also are being challenged, and we have not taken the time to recognize these challenges and to acknowledge our responsibility in these instances. We have run out of the gate and into the world, but we have left behind some of the reasons we decided to take these paths. We need to stop and consider who we are and what we represent, and we need to accept the responsibility to continue to be what we claim to be, not just for the sake of consistency, but to protect our identity and the freedoms we have come to cherish.

One of the most common associations in the pagan community is the reference to "earth-based spirituality." We pride ourselves on our environmental concerns. We constantly say we're responsible for Mother Earth, but how many of us are fully involved in these concerns?

What do we mean when we say "earth-based"? What is the full range of this concept? Are we referencing only the parts that make us comfortable or that are easy to incorporate into our daily lives? Or are we looking at the full balance of nature and focusing on maintaining that balance across the board?

Being earth-based is not a matter of counting the trees, feeding the animals, conserving water, and protecting the environment. A much bigger segment of earth-based people populate the planet. We make more of an impact on the Earth in our everyday living than we can fix in decades spent at weekend seminars or pagan events. And most of it involves the human condition, which in turn affects water conservation, land management, and animal protection. I have seen people get more excited over animal abuse and take more action to prevent soil erosion than they do to prevent a child from going hungry.

Being in Community

I've worked with many communities in the northeast United States, and it is amazing to see the pockets of advancement that have been made in the past years with regard to growing real pagan communities.

We don't have many working models to point to as "successful," but we have some experimental communities of pagans who have banded together to form not just spiritual communities, but also cultural communities. I remember a discussion about a group that was looking at a co-op where they could purchase controlling shares and open it to their own community. Their plan included assisted living facilities for their elder membership. This was not a "free" project, but a project of hard-working pagans who are sharing and celebrating their diversity as well as looking at their responsibility toward their membership. There was some discussion of converting it to a "green" property, as well.

We have pagans living in smaller communities, either renting in the same facilities or purchasing property and housing as it becomes available on the market in certain areas. We have communal farms and green-earth communal projects. The problem is that most of these projects are experimental or the communities have not published their results. And some communities are not in constant communication with other communities, and other more extreme environmental communities are without power for tools like the Internet. It is only when we meet a member at an event and the discussion comes up that we learn that these experiments are happening.

In the meantime, smaller grass-roots groups are working with the occasional visitor to their community and keeping a record of services available and resources for the needs of these community members. You know these groups. They have names like the Pagans of (fill in the blank) County or the Witches of (insert name of city). There are working community groups that hold occasional events or a Pagan Night Out, and there will be groups that have information to share with the community. You will find these communities listed in the occult bookstores or esoteric shops and online at better-known pagan Web sites that list local groups.

These groups will have regular membership and floating members. Those floating members will be the occasional visitors or the pagans who have discovered they have a need and now are looking for someone to point them in the right direction. But how can we take care of these people, and how can we give them the information they need without dragging them out into the community they seem reluctant to join? Many people have had good cause over the years to be cautious.

Replace Wariness with Trust

Trust seems to be a factor in why people don't join communities. We can build trust with others by being available, being discrete, and being responsible. Being a source of reference information is also a good way to build trust. I remember one member of a local community group carried a binder with him at all times. This person had brochures, leaflets, and lists with names, addresses, and phone numbers to hand out to anyone who was interested in the local resources.

Lack of trust is a hard barrier to overcome within the pagan community. While we all speak of being responsible, we have seen many who are not. It is important to note that the lack of responsibility is not restricted to the pagan community; rather, it is a reflection of the times we live in. We see issues in all communities, which may be why so many pagans seem to shy away from community.

There is a lot to consider here in regard to how we want to progress as a culture, a community, and as a spiritual experience; and how we can improve the quality of life and the human condition for those within our community. In addressing the role of trust in communities, we need to also realize that resolution of these issues is not confined to the pagan community, but the human community as a whole.

Speak Out to Change the Status Quo

How can we be more responsible for the human condition, in general? It starts within each of us. It radiates out from our homes and moves out into greater and greater circles, like our magic, and it touches each person along the way. Discussion should begin within your groups, your covens, your organizations, and your families. I suggest that we look at how we each see our choices, our values, our independence, and our free will. Are we being responsible individuals and how much more can we extend those responsibilities to include the most important and cherished element that Mother Earth has produced—we, her children?

Boudica *is reviews editor and co-owner of* The Wiccan/Pagan Times *and owner of* The Zodiac Bistro, *both online publications. She is a high priestess with the Mystic Tradition Teaching Coven of Pennsylvania, Ohio, New Jersey, New York, and Maryland. Boudica is a guest speaker at many local and East Coast events. A former New Yorker, she now resides with her husband and six cats in Ohio.*

Illustrations: Kathleen Edwards

Wiccan Agreements

Danny Pharr

I am not Moses. I have not stood before a burning bush. I have not received from a jealous god Ten Commandments written in stone.

However, sitting in the stone circle outside my house, with a balefire burning on the night after the Summer Solstice, I considered the lack of acceptance among the general populace and the Christian faith of our Wiccan ways and beliefs. Even though most of the beliefs the Christians hold dear are rooted in pagan antiquity, and the same could be said for most of the major religions, they do not accept our religion.

And I wondered if those of us who follow the old ways, be they that of the Craft, Druids, Isians, and so forth, are unconsciously creating this reality simply through our choices, behaviors, and actions. More so, are we creating every aspect of our lives through our choices—in effect as an active part of evolution, which in some ways

makes each of us god-like. And I began to consider the rules that we say we live by and whether or not we truly abide them.

Our goddesses and gods would never command of us, but we do have "agreements." Regardless of what we call them, they are more than just good ideas to live by, they are the laws by which we govern our actions.

The Wiccan canon can be summarized in this rede:

Bide the Wiccan Rede ye must,
In perfect love, in perfect trust,
Eight words the Wiccan Rede fulfill,
And ye harm none, do what thou will.
Live ye must and let to live,
Fairly take and fairly give.
And wary one should always be,
To ever mind the Rule of Three.

As a practicing pagan, influenced so heavily by the Wiccan and Druid beliefs, I must first consider how my thoughts and my deeds affect me, my immediate world, and the larger world around me. This is part of the self-examination we all take before acting upon the realms of the Mighty Ones. What are my intentions and am I advancing those intentions in a manner conducive to the outcome desired and within the laws of my faith?

The act of setting an intention can be related to the fight between good and evil or, more to the point, between blessedness and the profane. There is no good or evil, at least not in our belief system; however, there are blessed acts and profane acts. These would be the acts that are in line with the natural order and those that are not, respectively.

I believe this is why the Rule of Three exists; it is part of the natural order. As we set out intentions and influence those around us, we are creating in that moment the energy we will receive back from the people we encounter. If we act blessedly and make choices on the side of righteousness, we will influence others to do the same and that is what we will receive from them in the future: an evolutionary act. The Rule of Three is a byproduct of evolution.

We are a part of evolution, we create our future; therefore, we are god-like. Of course, pagans have always felt close to their gods and goddesses; they are our friends, our brothers and sisters, and, at times, our uncles and aunts who look after us and foster us.

Choice promotes evolution. Intention influences attitudes, attitudes affect choices, a series of choices creates direction, direction creates outcomes, outcomes influence other choices and other people's intentions, which in turn affects their attitudes, choices, direction, outcomes, and still other people's intentions. Over time, the influence of one's original intention spreads across humanity with decreasing effectiveness as it reaches further and further, like a drop of water in a pond, sending ripples in all directions toward the shoreline. The first ripple, the one closest to the impact of the drop, is the tallest and strongest and has the most influence on the surrounding water molecules. As the ripples spread toward the edge of the pond, they flatten out, until they disappear.

Setting an intention and following the direction created by the intention influences the people that we come in contact with daily. And those people influence others, and they others, and so on, until the originating influence is diminished. This gradually reduced effect is counteracted by repetition.

When everyone is moving in the same direction, with the same intention and the same goals, amazing things can be accomplished. These amazing accomplishments affect a greater percentage of humanity than an individual effort, but an individual still has an affect. Evolution is a slow process of change on a global scale.

Setting intention begins with an idea. This idea is then nurtured into an ideal, whereupon a ritual is conceived and acted out to manifest this ideal into the world—to manipulate the future—to evolve. Ritual is our version of prayer; it's another method of talking to our goddesses, gods, and our higher selves. When the energy of many is unified into any form of prayer toward a common goal, that goal stands a much better chance of being achieved. Prayer works, in all its forms.

So are we pagans really so unlike our Christian brothers and sisters in our different faiths and our adherence to them? A certain commonality seems to exist in the laws by which we live our faiths. And, for all of our judgments, fears, and disfavor directed at the Christian's faith, and for theirs at us, I'm not sure that we bind ourselves to our faith any more or less than they do.

There must be reasons for our not accepting the Christian faith and for the Christian faith not accepting us. The light of common sense and logic should revel these reasons to be more substantial than emotion and tradition, more vital than a lack of self-worth manifesting as envy, more material than egocentric self-inflation through judgment, or more enlightened than just plain fear. Maybe the answer is in the rules of our two faiths.

Deconstructing Our Agreements

"In perfect love, in perfect trust" is one of the greatest ideals ever uttered from mankind's lips, and yet, is this ideal attainable in our community? It is an ideal to be strived for and worked toward; and, like most mysteries, a topic to meditate upon, but until every member finds their higher self and adopts an attitude of living in the moment, it is not attainable.

"And ye harm none, do what thou will" is the supreme of our laws, the highest of our ideals, that which sets the standard and shapes the rest. These eight words hold a monumental edict, and yet they are still open to interpretation, mostly due to the words "harm" and "none." Harm can be extended to include mental, physical, and spiritual injury, and it can be expanded to include financial injury or any act that results in injury to one's interests over time. These injuries can be made knowingly or unknowingly, with thoughts of malice or justice. And then there is the other word: none. Who or what does "none" include? Many would say that "none" includes both man and beast, others would say "none" means all forms of life, and still others might suggest "none" simply includes living humankind. For the purpose of this thesis, we will assume that "harm" refers to an intentional or preconceived act that causes injury, trauma, damage, or impairment in a physical or mental way, and "none" will be assumed to mean humankind. Otherwise, the ramifications of

these arguments will be so wide-ranging that we could never work our way through them.

"**Live ye must and let to live**" is more than the obvious. Though, "Live ye must" also refers to living a full life and "let to live," refers to living in the moment, without fear deterring one's choices, without future-tripping or past-dwelling.

"**Fairly take and fairly give**" is as much about self-care and dealing fairly with our inner emotional selves, as it is about fair dealings with others.

"**And wary one should always be, to ever mind the Rule of Three**" reaffirms the measure of justice that is the Rule of Three, which brings all my actions back to me threefold. And more than just actions and deeds, it is the intent of the action or deed. That which ye sow once, ye shall thrice reap.

Deconstructing the Ten Commandments

The Ten Commandments are written and organized a bit differently by the various factions abiding by the rules. What follows is the orthodox version.

1. I am the Lord your God. You shall have no other gods before me.

2. You shall not make for yourself an idol.

3. You shall not make wrongful use of the name of your God.

4. Remember the Sabbath and keep it holy.

5. Honor your father and mother.

6. You shall not murder.

7. You shall not commit adultery.

8. You shall not steal.

9. You shall not bear false witness against your neighbor.

10. You shall not covet your neighbor's house. You shall not covet your neighbor's wife.

In comparing these commandments to the Wiccan Rede, we first have to eliminate the commandments that are based in the jealousy that the Christian God freely admits to holding. Therefore, the first three have got to go. After that, the remaining commandments have some meaning.

"Remember the Sabbath and keep it holy." This could be as easily written, remember the sabbats and keep them holy. The difference here being: Our pagan version of holy means to honor rather than to somberly acknowledge.

"Honor your father and mother." This says to the pagan, one should honor Father Sky and Mother Earth, the God and the Goddess, the masculine and the feminine, or any of the many pairings we recognize.

"You shall not murder." This is limited to acts against persons by use of the word murder, but it falls under the overarching "And ye harm none, do what thou will" and also "Live ye must and let to live." The idea of murder can be expanded to an emotional or spiritual level as well.

"You shall not commit adultery." Although pagans honor the sexual union, we also honor each other. A married person indulging in sexual relations with someone other than their spouse is generally a malicious act when viewed from the point of view of the spouse. "And ye harm none, do what thou will." Adultery would be argued as harmful to some, including the participants.

"You shall not steal." Stealing was originally a reference to kidnapping. Regardless, stealing a person or stealing a person's possessions is harmful and therefore against our rede.

"You shall not bear false witness against your neighbor." The word neighbor could be limited to the people in one's community, but was likely written to include all mankind. Many pagans revere the knightly ways of old, including the knight's mandate: Speak the truth even if it means your death. Accordingly, the rede offers: Fairly take and fairly give. Fairness means truthfulness.

"You shall not covet your neighbor's house. You shall not covet your neighbor's wife." Coveting would fall under the rede as, "Live ye must and let to live," in the broader sense. If one spends his life wishing his life to be different, he will be creating a life without joy. Also, "perfect love" will exclude such desires.

Thus far in our examination, there is little difference between the Wiccan Rede and the Christian commandments, except for the jealousy of their god. And the rede is broader in scope than the commandments, making the rede more difficult to fulfill. Maybe there are differences between the pagan ways and the Christian's seven virtues and deadly sins.

The seven deadly sins all have one thing in common—they interfere with a person's ability to be close to the Divine, keeping one instead connected to the earthly realm. They also have this same affect in common with every act that is not blessedly intended.

The seven deadly sins and the seven virtues also seem to fall within the bounds of our faith. The sins seem to be examples of the commandments, and the virtues seem to be examples of how to live while expelling sin. The Wiccan Rede gives us ideals to achieve; no rules, no punishments, only acknowledging the natural order of things. And yet, the differences between our faiths seem minimal.

"Pride" is the mother of all sins. Pride empowers the other sins. Pride, also known as Vanity, is acknowledging one's abilities or achievements to such an excessive degree that Grace has no foothold. "Prudence" is a virtue that stands in the face of pride. These fall within the "Fairly take and fairly give" act of the rede. Pride negates fairness, and prudence promotes it.

"Envy" is the excessive wanting of that which belongs to another, be it societal status, material wealth, innate ability, physical attributes, or any other jealousy. It is easy to see how Pride could spawn envy. I do find it contradictory that a jealous god would command his followers to avoid jealousy, but that may be a topic for another day. Justice is the virtue that best contradicts envy. According to Plato, a just individual is someone who is governed by reason rather than passion or ambition. Again, "Fairly take and fairly give" applies here.

"Gluttony" is extraordinary consumption beyond what the body actually needs to thrive, thus depriving the body of the prosperity of life. "Live ye must and let to live" is the Wiccan response to gluttony. Yes, we must eat to live, but must moderate eating to let ourselves live to the maximum. Temperance is the Christian virtue opposing gluttony—all things in moderation.

"Lust" is an unreasonable hunger for physical pleasures. This usually refers to sex, but, can be applied to any physical pleasure. "Faith" is the virtuous counterpoint to lust. In one's faith the spirit is elevated and can turn away from the physical wants of the body. Sex is a part of the natural order and therefore welcomed in the pagan faith. And sex is not the problem; it is the excessive wanting that is at issue. Lust is much like greed and gluttony and would be acted upon by equally by our ideals.

Choice is always present. We always have choice in everything we do.

"Wrath" is the opposite of "Hope," but curiously wrath and hope are manifested from the same source, which is fear. Wrath is the inordinate feelings of anger or hatred, coupled with a desire for revenge. Anger is generally manifested by fear of one or many future possibilities, such as embarrassment, pain, death, loss, etc. Hope is desire that something better will occur if one perseveres. Hope is also based in fear, the fear that the present situation is the best it will ever be. "In perfect love, in perfect trust" resolves the issues of wrath and hope.

"Avarice," or greed, is offset by "Charity." Avarice is the desire for material wealth or gain, ignoring the realm of the spiritual. It is also called "covetousness." Charity, of course, is the act of freely giving of oneself or one's possessions. "Fairly take and fairly give."

"Sloth," in its most common usage, is the avoidance of physical work, although it can also be defined as the refusal to put one's talents into use or, basically, laziness. Sloth originally was conceived as sadness because of one's refusal to accept the joys of their god by having an apathetic spirituality creating discontent. "Fortitude" is a mental strength that promotes endurance. Applying fortitude to a situation helps by removing obstacles from one's journey. This virtue is often the savior of the hero, drawing from it his will to go on in the face of fear. "In perfect love, in perfect trust" is the pagan answer to Sloth and the correspondent to Fortitude.

Once again we see that there is very little difference between the Christian mandates and the pagan ideals, except, perhaps, in the manner they are presented and in the manner in which followers are encouraged to adopt the practices. We truly do seem to be more alike than we are different. We want the same things, have similar spiritual goals, but are motivated differently. The difference appears to be choice.

Choice is always present. We always have choice in everything we do. To assume or believe otherwise makes us victims. Sometimes our choices aren't what we would prefer, but we always have choice, even in the worst cases. The metaphor might be choosing to die standing or to die kneeling.

Christians choose whether or not to follow decrees with very specific limitations on behavior, and torturous consequences for themselves and their progeny and heirs for not behaving; pagans choose whether or not to live in a manner of constant choice between blessedness or profanity and accept the triple consequences of either path for themselves and, ultimately, humanity. As we have already shown, every individual action affects the future and therefore evolution, so faith's followers are manifesting the future in their choices. Christians seem to have less personal responsibility as they are theoretically following fairly rigid rules that are intended to create a utopian afterlife; whereas, pagans have great personal responsibility as their daily choices are paradisaical in their evolutionary nature.

I believe we have affirmatively answered the question of creating our own reality. We have also come to the conclusion that Christians and pagans are basically the same in the canonic tenets of their faiths.

All that remains is to decide if our lack of acceptance by the Christian faith is of our creation, and the truthful answer to that question is: "It doesn't matter." We already know that we create every part of our life experience. So, of course we create our own lack of acceptance. But what is really most important here is not that we manifest our future, but, without regard for the past, what future we manifest. In other words, are we truly living our faith and striving to achieve the ideals set forth in the Wiccan Rede.

Many will argue that this whole treatise is based on a desire to be accepted by the Christians that makes us victims, expecting something from someone else, and that this is a false desire. Overall, pagans do not care if they are accepted by anyone, that we are outside of normal society, that we have our own ways. And to this argument, I agree, mostly. However, acceptance, in this discussion, is more about community than it is ego. We are a communal people, not just pagans, but people in general, and we seek community in our various ways; and a functional community is based on the similarities of the members.

The final question, do we actually live our faith? The answer has to be "no." But because the Wiccan faith is based on a set of ideals that are for the most part unattainable at this point in our evolution, degrees of attainment must be considered. The pre-Christian Celts, some of our magical ancestors, included, as a part of their dogma this tenet: "It's the journey, not the destination."

When considering the journey, a life path, all one can do is to take each step, minute by minute, day by day, and do what one is capable of doing. Every day that we strive to embody the ideals of our faith is a day that we are closer to our Goddesses and Gods, and after

all, that is the point: bring together the realm of the Mighty Ones and the realm of the mundane, in each of us daily. In that way, we will have achieved paradise on earth.

The solution to acceptance by those of the Christian faith, more importantly, acceptance in the world at large, and even more importantly still, acceptance of everyone by everyone, is living our faith. Students of theology often find that the major religions have similar goals for human behavior and similar moral boundaries. Assuming this to be true, and if everyone lived their faith, if everyone was a shining example of a "good person," a person of blessed intentions and actions, we would all find that we are basically good, blessed, moral people, respecting one another. In this utopian place, only joy and happiness would exist. Choose to be happy.

If the Wiccan Rede is rewritten per our redefined terms and in modern language, it might look like this:

> *Do whatever you choose, as long as*
> *you don't knowingly or intentionally*
> *cause physical or mental injury, trauma,*
> *damage, or impairment*
> *to any other living human.*

Even with this limited definition, to bide this law, one must be ever vigilant not to adversely affect the life of another in any negative way, including while plainly taking care of oneself.

Danny Pharr *is an author and a master firewalk instructor. He founded Wings of Fire Seminars to provide individuals with a safe environment to discover and engage in life-changing experiences. His first book , The Moon and Everyday Living, was published by Llewellyn in 2000.*

Illustrations: Tim Foley

Witchy Living

DAY-BY-DAY WITCHCRAFT

Sustainable Witchcraft

Melanie Harris

Green living can do more than protect the planet and stave off eco-guilt. The actions we take and the choices we make to minimize damage to the environment can give the witch new power, improve magical ability, and offer creative formats for spellwork. If we want to work well with the natural elements and energies we use in magic, we must have a good relationship with those forces, a mutual willingness to cooperate founded on shared experience, trust, caring, and respect. Trashing the Earth and then calling on those same forces to help you with your magic is like asking an enemy for a favor. Through choices that ensure our personal Craft has a positive impact on the environment, and through actions that turn everyday green-living activities into opportunities for magic, we become nature's true friend, and friendship with nature is the foundation of magical expertise.

We witches tend to be pretty in tune with the environment, yet from the stones and herbs that we use in our fondness for bonfires, the tools and traditions of magic can sometimes actually hurt the world around us. The informed witch can reduce the risk of accidentally damaging her alliance with nature by choosing to avoid those magical products and practices that are not sustainable.

When buying incense, essential oils, or dried herbs, for instance, know what you're getting and where it came from. The global herb trade has a rather dark underbelly. For example, illegal harvesting and overharvesting of sandalwood has damaged ecosystems in India and Australia. Many herbal products suppliers spray their crops with toxic chemicals or add synthetic ingredients to their essential oil blends. We don't contribute to the problems if, instead, we choose natural, pure products that are grown, picked, and processed without causing a lot of environmental damage. We can take more care when we gather wild plants, too. Be sparing and learn to identify native species. Taking more acorns than you need or uprooting an endangered plant in your local forest can threaten biodiversity.

Stones and metals can also come to us with a heavy environmental cost. Most mining operations scar the land and leach chemicals into the soil and water, thereby leaving a lasting negative impact. Find out where and how stones and metals are produced, and you will be empowered to buy products that are more eco-friendly and that pack a stronger magical punch. A quartz crystal that you found and carefully collected yourself will naturally contain more magical energy than a quartz crystal that came to you through a mining operation that devastated the Earth.

Another staple of the Craft, the outdoor fire, emits large amounts of air pollution, but you need not extinguish that sabbat fire completely. There are ways to reduce the amount of polluting smoke put out by a fire. First of all, burn only fallen, dry, dead wood. Green wood, or wood that has been treated with paints or other chemicals, releases more pollutants into the air. Limit the size and frequency of your fires, and follow all regulations.

Witchcraft can also take its toll on the water supply. When you make water-based brews and potions, use only as much water as is necessary for the recipe. Collect and use dew or rainwater for non-ingestible blends. If it's not too soapy, you can even recycle the water from a magical bath, using it to nourish the plants in your garden or to clean and purify ritual tools.

Sustainable witchcraft is not just about greening up your magic, though. It's also a way to work magic through your eco-conscious activities. Try these new methods of modern magic, and you will help yourself as you help the Earth.

Recycling Spell

Sorting those soda cans and old newspapers into the recycling bin doesn't have to be a chore. It can be a new way to work spiritual transformation magic. If you're feeling downtrodden and in need of a boost, feel your frustrations and doubts and send those energies into the recyclables. Think about the recycling process, the way that the old becomes the new, and envision yourself reborn, free of negativity and full of fresh ideas. Say an affirmation, such as "Just as this can will be recycled into something new, so may my stale mindset be transformed into inspiration."

Banish the Trash Charm

Picking up litter can be the vehicle for a powerful banishing charm. Be it insecurities, a bad habit, bad luck, or even a pimple, whatever you wish to cast aside will be out of your life a lot sooner with the help of the Banish the Trash charm. When you see some litter, visualize the thing you wish to banish and send this image into the trash. Keep your thoughts firm, peaceful, and positive. As you toss each piece of litter into the trash bag, speak some words of banishment; a simple "Be gone!" will do.

Magical Preparation Ritual

Your personal power and your affinity with nature's magical energies will be strengthened if you use as little water, fuel, and electricity as possible in the days leading up to an important spellcasting or other sacred time. Enjoy a lights-off divination or meditation session every evening, put on your walking shoes, see how fast you can take a shower. Push yourself to conserve the Earth's resources as much as you can, and the forces of nature will lend you their power when it comes time to work your magic.

Repairing Ritual

Restoring a section of depleted land can help a witch work through old emotional scars and emerge renewed. Find an area that needs help, and set aside some time each week to go to the place and work on restoring the natural ecosystem. You will likely need to do a combination of things, such as digging terraces to prevent erosion, spreading compost to add nutrients to the soil, and planting native plants to restore natural vegetation.

As you're working on the land, think through the memories that continue to upset you. When you are ready to let go of an old hurt, bury it in the ground. Place your palm firmly on the dirt and say, "Enough!" As you continue to nurture and replenish the land, you will work through your emotions and find closure, peace, and renewal.

Animal-friend Magic

You can develop a closer relationship with your spirit animal or real-life familiar by helping other animals of their species. For instance, if a cat is your familiar, you might give a bag of pet food to the local cat shelter, or organize a community seminar to educate people about the needs of cats. If your spirit animal is the gorilla, you might offer your skills to causes that support gorillas and their habitats. You could organize a benefit concert to collect money to help protect the rain forest. You could volunteer to help with fundraising, or design a brochure or campaign poster to generate public interest.

When you generously offer your unique talents and skills to help animals thrive, those animals will be happy to help along your magic.

These guidelines, spells, and rituals can enrich your Craft and befriend the Earth. By incorporating magic into your green living, and incorporating green living into your magic, you will enjoy the full benefits of sustainable witchcraft: more power, more methods for spellwork, and a stronger bond between magic, person, and planet.

Melanie Harris *is the founder of* United Witches, *a global coven for magical people of all paths. An advocate for personalized magic and an experienced tarot reader, she has written for many pagan and esoteric publications including* Tarot Reflections, *the* Llewellyn Journal, Pentacle Magazine, *and* Circle Magazine.

Illustrations: Kathleen Edwards

Cyber Altars: Using New Technology in Traditional Ways

Lisa McSherry

I grew up in a house full of altars. My mother would probably disagree with calling them altars, but I remember that every flat surface in the house had a grouping of special objects. Candles in unusual holders sat next to the flowering violets and small portraits of family members in the hall. Pottery forms that she created with love shared space with crystals and shells in the living room. It seemed like every season she would rearrange the furniture, and the altars would be changed, moved, reformed into new combinations. Those experiences imparted a key lesson to me, which was that altars have been with us for thousands of years, bringing the sacred into our homes in personal, tangible ways.

Nowadays, it may seem odd that most of my ritual work is performed at a cyber altar, but I see it as the next step, a new direction to take the notion of sacred and incorporate it into our lives. Many of us use computers daily, so why shouldn't we bring them into our sacred circles?

In her book *Altars*, Denise Linn said, "Since time immemorial, the primary function of altars and shrines has been to provide sacred and holy places amid the ordinary reality of life." The process of transforming a computer into an altar has the potential to completely change how we use them and what can be produced. Writers, for example, probably use a computer for most of their work of writing, editing, and communicating with editors and publishers. If we transformed our otherwise mundane computers into altars to creativity, who knows what the Muse will bring to us or how much deeper into the creative flow we will go.

That is only one form of cyber altar, however. There are also Web pages, such as those found at www.SpiralGoddess.com, that act as shrines to particular divinities. The Spiral Goddess site also has a place where you can use graphics they have designed to build your own cyber altar, which can be saved to your own computer and admired later. Other cyber altars worship cultural icons. The one for Tori Amos has a place to light a candle and speak a few words (recorded forever on the Internet). Other cyber altars allow you to light a candle in remembrance of those who have passed on, or as a token of appreciation for lessons learned (usually through hardship).

There are astral altars as well, and that is where I do a large portion of my ritual work. Traditionally, an astral altar has been a place that is visualized and manifested within our own minds, usually as part of a temple or place of power. In my work, the astral altar is

where my coven and class meet to hold rituals online. For the coven, the altar is quite specific in form as it is part of a larger structure
within which we worship. For the class, the altar varies according to
perspective and ability.

As part of the process of preparing for our cyber rituals, we transform
our work area (the physical location of the computer) into an altar. Each
of us creates private sacred space from which we link to one another in
cyberspace to create a vast sphere of energetic connections.

Since we are unique, we each have our own way of preparing our
sacred space. In my case, I disassemble my main altar and set it up
again on my desk (mirroring the process in reverse after the ritual

is complete). Others in the group have two altars, a main altar and a second one for cyber rituals, or their permanent altar is next to their desk. When they cast their personal circles, they include both their desk and altar. One member of Jaguar Moon has her permanent altar in an adjoining room, against the same wall as her computer desk. She simply casts a circle big enough to enclose both spaces through the wall.

Setting Up Your Cyber Altar

Setting up a cyber altar will, of course, have much to do with a variety of factors: desk size, what you feel is necessary for ritual, how your desk is laid out, and so on. There are a few recommendations I can offer. Make sure that nothing hot is placed near either yourself or any electronics, and keep smoke or other foreign substances (like soap bubbles) away from the CPU. You can easily type and move objects on your altar as appropriate for the ritual.

As with any altar, make sure that the items you place there are symbolic of the elements, the Deity, as well as anything specific to the ritual being performed. Although you may not actually use all of the tools during a cyber ritual, having them present adds to the sense of the sacred and honors the elements present. Laying down an altar cloth and using incense and candles to create a sense of mood are wonderful additions.

My altar is shaped like an equal-armed L and fits perfectly into a corner, which allows me to set up my altar in either the north or the east. Because of its shape, I can place an altar cloth over one side, lay my tools out, light candles around the room, and I am ready to go. (Of course, I also make sure the other section is cleared of distracting elements.) My cats like to lie in the cleared desk area during my rituals and occasionally move to my lap.

To make your computer a cyber altar can be as complicated or simple a task as you want to make it, depending on your skill, desire, and creativity. At the simplest level, change your screen image to something that evokes a sacred or magickal response in you. Change it with the seasons, the sabbats, every week, or anytime you are working magick. One of my personal favorites is changing passwords to evoke magickal responses. Instead of having "8uyC9" as your password, make it "lovinG" or "@bunDance". Each time you type those words, you will create a trigger to send a moment of energy toward manifesting them into your life.

If that doesn't feel like enough, transform the area around your computer into an altar, with the monitor as the center (or just a component, whichever feels more correct). Take a moment to sit in silence at your desk. Relax and imagine yourself laughing and in a constant state of joy. Feel the sparkle of creative juices flowing through you. Enjoy that feeling for as long as you wish, and then open your eyes. Look around you and throughout your life for objects that symbolize creativity for you. You might use jars of paint brushes, coloring pens, or pencils; images of inspiring works (your own or others'); or scraps of paper with inspirational quotes or creative doodles taped all over the monitor.

You'll be pleasantly surprised how transforming your computer space into a sacred space helps creative energy flow over into your other work. The novelist Anne Rice writes quotes on her monitor when she writes a new book, and she starts with a fresh monitor with each new project. I've seen bubble soap in pottery jars, kitchen utensils in a cheese grater, crazy quilt scraps pinned to paper, notebooks covered in special fabric, colored ink pens attached by long ribbons, and many other unique collections. Anything goes—if it pleases you, use it.

My mother's altars opened the door for me; her wisdom and creativity has flowed throughout my life ever since. Now that she uses a computer, it pleases me that she follows my example and creates sacred space every time she types her password.

REFERENCES

Cunningham, Nancy Brady, and Denise Geddes. A Book of Women's Altars: How to Create Sacred Spaces for Art, Worship, Solace, Celebration. Red Wheel, Boston, 2002.

Linn, Denise. *Altars: Bringing Sacred Shrines Into Your Everyday Life.* Ballantine Wellspring, New York, 1999.

WEB SITES

http://www.spiralgoddess.com/MyOwnAltar.html
http://www.spiralgoddess.com/
http://www.webcoves.com/circles/brighid.html
http://members.aol.com/redselchie/altar/altar.html
http://www.geocities.com/sunsetstrip/frontrow/1814/torialtaradd.
  html

Lisa McSherry *has been a practicing witch for almost thirty years and has led a coven (www.jaguarmoon.org) for almost ten. She is the author of* The Virtual Pagan: Exploring Wicca and Paganism Through the Internet *(Weiser, 2002) and* Magickal Connections: Creating a Lasting and Healthy Spiritual Group *(New Page, 2007). The owner of Facing North: A Community Resource (www.facingnorth.net), she can be reached at: lisa@cybercoven.org*

Illustrations: Rik Olson

The Compact Witch: Crafting Rituals in Small Spaces

Magenta Griffith

You love living in the city, but the only apartment you can afford is tiny, or you have to share it with three other people. You don't have nine feet in which to draw a circle, unless your bed is in the middle. What's a witch to do?

One answer is to start thinking small, and a good starting point is to remember that the most important part of being a witch is what is going on inside your head and heart. A witch doesn't need space as much as time and attention. All the tools in the world won't make up for a lack of focus.

Thinking Outside the Space

The circle does not have to be drawn by physically walking around the room. While it's often easier to visualize a circle when you have actually walked the boundaries, you don't have to physically move through the space each time. (It might help if you walk the boundary of the circle once, very deliberately.) If you have a roommate, do this when they are out and don't intrude on their space. It's better the circle is more of an oval than to extend it past your personal area. Since you may have to move furniture to set up ritual space, portable items, like futons and folding chairs, are a plus under these circumstances.

The altar can be a small folding table, the kind just large enough for a dinner plate. Use small versions of the usual tools—a pocketknife as an athame, a doll's goblet as chalice. A small stone—perhaps a small semiprecious stone—can symbolize earth. One advantage of working small is that a small gem is more affordable than a large one. If you wish to use salt to symbolize earth, see if you can find an old-fashioned salt dish. Small candles, such as birthday candles, have the advantage of burning quickly (concentrating the whole time a candle is lighted is far easier with a tiny candle). For statues of the Goddess and the God, figures etched in stones or meant for jewelry, work quite well. If nothing is fragile, put your altar components in an altar cloth for storage. Otherwise, store everything in the same box or drawer when you aren't working magic.

The top of a dresser or bureau can also be used for altar space. Store the items you might usually have on top of your dresser in a drawer, and put the Goddess statue and tools on top if you have the privacy to leave it out all the time. If you can, use a drawer exclusively for your ritual storage, or use a divider if your dresser drawers are large. Small hanging shelves can be used to hold your witchcraft materials. One witch I know has a set of four shelves hanging on the wall that hold the items for fire, water, earth, and air.

To cut down on the amount of storage you need, find one or two types of incense and use those for all your rituals. Use votive candles, instead of pillar candles or tapers. Votives are also safer in a small space as the container limits the flame. A sword is imprac-

tical to cast the circle in a small space, so use a small knife, or even better, a wand or a feather—anything that you can use to direct energy. You may have to do without quarter candles, since they can be a hazard in a cramped space. Pictures on the walls to symbolize the directions can work quite nicely. For south, use a picture of a fire or volcano; for water, use a picture of the ocean or a waterfall.

If you don't have an understanding roommate, be polite, and look for another place to live if you can. You can also search for places other than your home to do rituals. A study carrel at school might work if it has no windows and a door that locks. Bring in what tools you need in a backpack, and do your rituals quickly and quietly under these circumstances. Make sure you remove all traces of the ritual. Under this circumstance, don't use candles or incense.

Better yet, look for a park or other green space to perform rituals. The best Full Moon rituals are done outside facing the Full Moon, weather permitting, of course. This is also the best solution for group work if no one has a large indoor space. You can have room to move around more freely outside, but find out the rules of the place in advance, so you don't stay past closing and get into trouble.

If a lack of privacy is part of your limits, remember that in times past, some witches had to disguise all their tools. A witch's athame was stored in the kitchen with other knives, for example, and the chalice might be a particularly beautiful goblet. Use only items that you would normally have in your living space. As with rituals held outdoors, learn to either keep your voice low or not say anything out loud.

For a while, my work was literally in the closet. I lived in a one room apartment and had very little space, but it had two small closets. One closet housed my altar, which rested on an orange crate. When I wanted to do a ritual, I opened the closet door; when I was finished, I closed it. This kept my ritual regalia apart from my mundane stuff and meant I didn't have to worry about a casual visitor knowing I was a witch.

Most witches end their rituals with cakes and wine. This does not have to be taken literally. Cookies or mini-muffins work well for "cakes," and "wine" can be any beverage that seems right to you. If you aren't supposed to have alcohol, whether it be for legal or health reasons, fruit juice or spring water is fine. It is a good idea to eat something at the end of the ritual to help you ground.

Remember that the magic happens inside of you, so don't be held back by the limits of your living quarters. Being able to work witchcraft under less than ideal conditions can be good practice, and it's not the tools that make the witch, but the witch that brings the tools to life.

Magenta Griffith *has been a witch more than 30 years and a high priestess for more than twenty years. She is a founding member of the coven Prodea, which has been celebrating rituals since 1980, as well as being a member of various pagan organizations such as Covenant of the Goddess. She presents classes and workshops at a variety of events around the Midwest. She shares her home with a small black cat and a large collection of books.*

Illustrations: Tim Foley

Magical Play: Unlocking the Doors of Magical Creativity

Shirley Lenhard

In many of the online pagan forums, there are some recurring themes with respect to magic that, to me, are disturbing. Many write that magic is something that must be worked at with serious intention and strict adherence to guidelines and rules; that there is no time for "fluff" or anything other than serious-minded hard work. Others write that the efficacy of magic is outside of their experiences and is something that must be harnessed as if it were a fleeting, unknown force instead of an energy that resonates from within. I've seen articles that are verbose, lengthy, and full of scientific experimentation, permutations, while being devoid of any humanistic ideals. Quite simply, many magical practitioners seem to have forgotten the simplicity of magic, or they have outright abandoned its simplicity for the studious realms of magic. However, at the end of the day, even the highest ceremonial magician is a simple human being who is capable of nothing more or less than any other human being. I believe my life is an entire miracle and totally is filled with magical occurrences. I communicate, I feel, I act, I think, I reason, I live—I am the embodiment of energy. That, to me, is the raw essence of magic.

For me, every utterance is a curse or blessing, every intentional act is a spell cast, every THING in my world contains a modicum of magical influence and energy because it was either conceived or

believed and ultimately achieved by me. I believe that the efficacy of magic lies within each and every practitioner and that magic is a gift to each soul incarnated.

We grow and mature, and we often forget about the simplicity of long summer days when we played outside and could create entire kingdoms out of cardboard boxes. We trade the magic of childhood for the stark reality of being an adult. Why do we do this? It isn't a law, and there is no sanction for bringing forth and remembering the inner child who yearns for magic in every detail of life. Young children have no problem with imagination, with creating a world of their own in which magical creatures exist and where magical acts are performed at the blink of an eye. Young children reside in a place that is filled to capacity with innocence and magic. They are capable, in their innocence, of great acts of kindness, and they have an abundance of awe at the simple things that life has to offer. As we all grow older and experience the ups and downs of the daily grind, we tend to lose that capacity to find the innocence, to recognize the simplest forms of magic. We become bogged down in the mundane—paying bills, finding gainful employment, and raising a family—and fail to recognize that there is magic even in the mundane. We simply have to give ourselves permission to see the lighter side of life and to incorporate play into our magical practices.

Play Has Its Benefits

In order for me to consider my magical practice a success, I find it beneficial to play, to find the child within and to invite her out to get dirty, to laugh, to color, to stomp in a rain puddle, or to recall the magic of being without a care in the world. I buy crayons—lots of crayons—and I often sit for hours on the floor scribbling and coloring and making odd shapes and designs. On one particular coloring jaunt, I discovered a calming effect that came from the colorful circles I had placed upon the paper. I turned the paper and began to notice a theme and before I recognized what I was doing, I was actually focusing on the feeling of the color and the gentle slope of the arcs. Before long I realized that I had created my own personal mandala.

A mandala is a design made of geometric symbols used in varying combinations and colors. I have often used a formal mandala, made by someone else, in meditation. The mandala is useful for focusing on the center, working outward along the contours, feeling the emotions emitted from the color combinations, and entering into the meditative state with a purpose to resolve an issue or relax the soul

and mind. When I focus on a mandala in meditation, the symbolism expressed by the mandala is impressed upon my subconscious mind; and in that state of meditation, I am able to prepare a sacred space in which I feel absolutely free to explore the inner child.

When I regularly use a mandala for meditation, it affects powerful, positive changes and growth in my practice. For instance, the color purple elicits from me a calming effect; it brings about a higher atunement to the spiritual side of my practice and assists in grounding me, which helps me to explore the emotions or issues that bring me to meditation. Invariably, I will reach for the color purple first, and the natural progression of colors and the patterns that unfold are the keys to unlocking the door of my subconscious and allowing the flow of inner peace to unfold through color and symmetry.

When a meditation session on a handcrafted mandala has been completed, I hang my mandala from a conspicuous place in my home as a reminder that the child within yearns to play. In that sphere of play, in that sacred space of meditation, all peace is found. The mandala serves as the means to reach a high meditative state; its calming effect on the psyche helps bring to light problems or issues, and the resolution is often found on the other side of the meditation. Having a self-created piece of art in the form of a mandala hanging conspicuously in my home also serves as a reminder of the innocence of play, the magic of a simpler time, and the memory that peace is attainable.

When was the last time that you climbed a tree? When was that? For me, it was a few weeks ago. I was walking in a local park and I could not shake the feeling that I was being drawn along a different path than I had ever taken in that particular park. I went with the feeling and was eventually led to a huge oak tree with low branches. I shrugged my shoulders and took off toward the tree, gaining speed, and I literally leapt onto the lower branches and hoisted myself up. I climbed less than halfway up the tree and found a place to nestle against the mighty trunk.

There was a gentle breeze up there among the limbs and leaves, an indignant pair of purple-throated finches, and a few ants. I rested my head against the trunk and wrapped one arm around its greatness, and I listened. I listened to the history of a former acorn turned mighty oak, and I realized that this tree was here long before me and would likely be here long after me. I asked for strength and for solid and deep roots for my family to thrive; and I felt the response in the stability of the branches that held my weight. I placed an offering of pennies on the tree's branches as I climbed down. When I reached the bottom, I found a twisted branch that I picked up and carried home.

Later, I fashioned the branch into a wand that I lovingly use as a reminder of the gift of strength and fortitude.

Climbing trees, while definitely a fete for the younger generations, is not prohibited simply because we have reached a certain chronological age. In fact, sitting in the boughs of that mighty oak, I was humbled by the fact that I could still be called to run, to feel the wind in my hair, to move my legs swiftly, and to scurry up a tree without any thought as to my age. It was both liberating and humbling to stand beneath that mighty oak and feel the youth of my forty-three years in that magical moment and to be thankful that I received this subtle reminder that magic abounds in the mundane act of climbing a tree.

Working with the Elements

I have noticed the more simplistic parts of the elements through elemental journeying and incorporating the aspects of each element into my path and welcomed them into my life. I have also come to realize that the element of water elicits a very innocent playfulness from me. Rainwater that gathers into puddles in parking lots, rain water that gathers in the street in front of my home, is a mirror into long humid southern days of my childhood that I spent singing and dancing in the rain. I have been known to run to my closet in search of rain boots and then scramble outside to stomp through rain puddles with great energy. The act of plodding through a puddle of freshly fallen rainwater is an act of innocence that is not easily lost once you rediscover it and the inner child who wants to come out to play!

Water is used in many of my own cleansing rituals, and on days when the rain has been consistent and soft, I use the time to reflect on the parts of my life that require cleansing. Then I proceed to dance and sing through freshly fallen rainwater for a ritual cleansing. The simplicity of being barefoot and singing as I visualize the

water washing away and cleansing my walk prepares me for a simpler way of living in the coming days. It restores and provides me with renewed confidence through natural cleansing.

There have been many such instances when child's play has revealed great gifts and wonderful and sage insight into matters that previously seemed like insurmountable obstacles in my adult life. I believe that it is the simplicity of the act that brings such bountiful rewards. Keeping it simple, incorporating play into my magical practice, and recognizing that there is magic in everything is, for me, the key to a successful magical practice.

High ceremonial magic does have its place in the pagan world, but everyone—even those high ceremonial magicians—would do well not to forget from whence they came. We all started out as children, born with an inherent sense of play, an innate feel for magic. We would do ourselves a great disservice if we lost the ability to be young at heart and forget how to breathe a fresh breath of youthfulness into our practices.

While there is a time and place for everything, I encourage everyone to stomp through a rain puddle and not to simply pass it by without so much as a glance. If you find a crayon, pick it up and color with it. If you have clay, mold it and shape it; and climb the tree. Remember to play. Remember that energy is the raw essence of magic, and children are a wealth of energy! Life is what you make of it, and magic is all around you. And when you read the labels that say "For ages 5 and up," that includes you!

Shirley Lenhard *holds a degree in psychology and has been a solitary witch for over twenty years. She works in the legal field by day and spends her free time playing, reading, handcrafting, gardening, and writing. She currently lives in New England with her devoted husband and their silly little dog, Pagan.*

Illustrations: Tina Fong

Shaman In the Streets

Mama Donna Henes

There used to be a person whose work was to keep track of the seasons: to cite the cycles in order to secure a celestial continuity. But in today's modern world there is no job description for what I do. For thirty-five years I have served as an urban shaman and eco-ceremonialist. I have produced hundreds of public participatory events and seasonal celebrations in parks, plazas, museums, schools, and streets throughout the United States, Canada, and Europe.

As shaman in every culture have done, I create contemporary rituals for my community, which I consider to be all of humanity. My role is that of catalyst. I organize and officiate innovative, de-mystified, nondenominational ceremonial systems for creative public interaction, celebration, and communion.

I work to facilitate nonthreatening, transformative ways for people to interrelate with each other, their own deepest and best selves, and the entire universe. This unifying involvement creates an energetically joined conceptual web—a communication network that connects us all at our cosmic center.

My intention is to create a magical, exhilarating, and involving atmosphere where regard, respect, and reverence rule and thereby inspire a sense of trust and safety so that truly sincere participation can occur. My rituals are very public and very participatory, with as many as several thousand people—folks of all stripes, hues, ages, and sects; initiates, strangers, and passersby, alike—coming together in a collective sharing of spirit.

People crave connection and thirst for a spiritual bond that can free them from the alienation of the modern world.

It is my special concern to offer significant and relevant ways for urban people to observe and participate in the wondrous workings of the world around us. The vast majority of the population of the planet today dwells in sprawling, paved, sound and light-polluted megalopolises. We are disenfranchised from the natural world, which is itself in danger of disappearing.

Despite what most of us have learned of the solar system as children, it is difficult to remember in an urban environment that we are rotating and revolving and spinning through space at a terrific speed—all at the same time. We are part of and, at the same time, painfully apart from the plan and patterns of the cosmos.

To remedy this sorry disconnect I have designed and, for the past three and a half decades, performed a series of "Celestially Auspicious Occasions," a term I coined to denote key occurrences of the universal cycles, which are the basis of the special holidays and holy days celebrated by people of every culture throughout time. These include the solstices and equinoxes, the four cross-quarter days that divide each season in half, the Full and New Moons, eclipses, and other significant heavenly phenomena.

My base, my center, you might say, is New York City, the capital of the world, where I am widely regarded as "The Unofficial Commissioner of Public Spirit of New York City" (so dubbed by *The New Yorker* magazine). But this grand tribute has not always been the case.

When I first started my professional shamanic practice all those years ago, the most common reaction I saw to my work was people rolling their eyes. People would sigh and look up to the sky as if searching the heavens for a nice, rational, normal person to talk to, instead of the kook I was perceived to be.

"Oh, Donna!" they would exclaim at each mention of energy or spirit. Their response, though, was more a jocular acceptance of my endearing weirdness than it was disdainful, insolent, or rude. I have to say that despite whatever anyone might have personally felt about what I was doing, the civic authorities, the general public, and the media have always treated me with great respect.

I suppose they could have been afraid that if they offended me, I would cast a nasty spell of toads or warts or rashes on them, but I prefer to think that beneath it all, there has been, from the very beginning, a certain acknowledgment and appreciation of the importance of ritual and celebration for the well-being of individuals and communities, alike.

People crave connection and thirst for a spiritual bond that can free them from the alienation of the modern world. Feeling a part of something greater than ourselves is very healing. We are all inundated with such high levels of stress and pressure that we often feel alone and isolated in a world consisting only of our own problems and worries. But we are not alone. We are inextricably interconnected to every other thing in the universe, and this realization gives us courage.

Well, the times sure have changed. Today, reverence for the Earth, green living, and environmental stewardship are chic. Meditation is mainstream and not just for Tibetan monks and hermits in caves. Community centers, schools, churches, offices, and gyms offer yoga and t'ai chi. Coaching, an outgrowth of the personal growth movement, is a major trend. Acupuncture, reiki, and energy healing are all enjoying popularity. The Goddess is invoked in razor blade and sanitary napkin commercials. And elegant ladies wear crystals hung on gold and silver chains.

These days I am hired to present special programs in the public schools about multicultural rituals for solstices and equinoxes, to lead drumming circles at bridal showers, to facilitate rituals for family occasions and milestones, to do house cleansings for real-estate agents, to perform jinx-breaking spells for building crews, and to offer blessings of newly constructed crypts at cemeteries.

I am the Grand Spirit Marshall of the world famous Greenwich Village Halloween Parade, where my Blessing Band leads the festivities with offerings of blessings for the streets, the city, and the two million spectators. And I also perform the Opening Blessing Ceremony of New York's Earth Day Festivities and major corporate-sponsored events. So what caused this enhancement of my image and official validation of my work?

I attribute this change of attitude to the massive amount of press coverage garnered by the hundreds of Celestially Auspicious Occasions that I have presented over the years. Thanks to the mainstream media, these public, participatory rituals celebrating each turn of the wheel of the year have gradually gained not just acceptance, but popular enthusiastic support of pagan Earth-honoring practices. The most renowned of these seasonal celebrations is Eggs on End: Standing on Ceremony, my Vernal Equinox ritual.

Soon after I started celebrating the seasons in public in the city on the Winter Solstice of 1975, a friend returned from Asia with an odd bit of equinoctial information. Apparently, in prerevolutionary China, it was customary to stand eggs on their end on the first day of spring. To do so would guarantee good luck for the entire year. What an intriguing image! On March 20, 1976, I and a merry little band of celebrants in Exotic Brooklyn went to a small park across the street from my home to prove it. Of course they stood.

The following year I mustered all of my trust in cosmic continuity and advertised a large public gathering to stand eggs up on the Spring Equinox at sunset on the waterfront in Battery Park in Manhattan. I assumed (and fervently prayed) that the eggs would stand again as they had the year before, as my ego was afraid of getting egg on my face. But of course they stood.

The event itself was astonishingly simple and has remained essentially the same for these thirty-five years. The site is always some towering landmark megalith, an urban Stonehenge. For nearly twenty years, my public altar was the plaza of the World Trade Center. A circle is cast, marked in day-glo orange ribbons donated by the power company (which is also in the business of creating energy!), thus transforming a secular public place into a sacred space. Scientific and mythic information sheets are handed out along with jelly eggs. Flares are lit to denote the number of days, weeks, months in a year. An orange laundry basket that contains 360 eggs is passed among the crowd.

Everyone takes an egg, and we all hold them up in the air together, pledging to walk on the Earth as if we were walking on eggs. We

promise anew, in honor of the season, to protect our fragile yet resilient planet and home. We count down the minutes to the equinox. And when the time is right, we stand our eggs in unison in a salute to spring. No matter how many people attend, the real event is always each single person feeling for her/his self what gravity and balance and equilibrium might mean.

Standing an egg on its end, feeling it as the yolk shifts inside to find its perfect point of balance, is like holding the entire universe in the palm of your hand. At the first moment of spring, the egg becomes the symbol of a new season, the renewal of life. Eggs On End: Standing On Ceremony is every bit a traditional pagan vernal fertility rite—a celebration of the return of green, growth, and light after the dark winter.

It is immaterial whether or not the egg can stand at any other time of the year (as some critics maintain). The important thing is to recognize the symbol, the season, the sky, and the kindred souls who share this magical moment with us. Cynicism magically disappears in the process of sincere participation. And, like the buds and birds of early spring, the participants, too, are renewed.

The morning after the first public "egguinx" event, a photo of 360 eggs standing against a brilliantly lit skyscraper background appeared in The New York Times. And the rest is history. Eggs On End: Standing On Ceremony has, from the first, captured the imagination of the media, as well as the general public. It is by far my most popular ritual. Whatever else I have done, or ever hope to do, in my life, I will always remain "the Egg Lady!"

This urban rite of spring has been featured on every television news network in the United States, as well as throughout Europe and Japan, and it has been written about in a myriad of national publications. Because of all the press coverage, the Spring Equinox is a familiar phrase in the popular vocabulary and is now a recognized holiday, noted everywhere on weather reports and on the news. Score one for Mother Earth!

The very first seasonal ritual that I ever performed was for the Winter Solstice in 1975. "Reverence to Her," a participatory chant to invoke the female forces of the universe present in all people, was held at Riis Park Beach in Queens, New York, at the exact time of the solstice, which was in the late evening.

The participants arrived in a caravan of cars, a school bus, and a truck filled with firewood. No sooner had we hauled the wood down to the beach and gathered in a circle, the cavalry arrived. Nine cars of city, state, and federal police screeched into the parking lot and descended upon us in a well-armed flurry with the intention of preventing us from lighting a fire and dispersing our crowd. Unbeknown to me, Riis Park Beach was not a city park, but part of the National Park Service, which protected it zealously. To this day I don't know how they knew we were there or our intentions.

... they commandeered our bus, herded us inside, posted two armed officers to guard us, and drove us to the 122nd precinct, where, after hours of detention, we were given a summons to appear in court.

I had prepared in advance a pyrotechnical extravaganza to usher in winter—a mixture of chemicals in my cauldron that were designed to self-ignite at the appointed solstice hour. And so they did. Right there, in front of the incredulous cops and the delighted solstice celebrants, was a spontaneous combustion at just the right moment! Even though our ceremony was interrupted and abridged, the essential ritual element had asserted itself and so we dutifully

hauled out the firewood and drove off into the winter night. Talk about a Celestially Auspicious Occasion!

Just about every Winter Solstice celebration that followed has had some sort of trial or trouble attached to it. The bus would get lost en route to some deserted beach, or the bus would break down in the middle of Greenwich Village or on the Verrazano Bridge. One year, the fully decorated bus was trapped in a parking lot by a car that had parked illegally right in front of the entrance. Year after year, it was always something. It is not easy, after all, to bring back the light on the darkest day of the year! Especially in the city.

It was my twenty-fourth annual Reverence to Her that ratcheted the Winter Solstice celebration up from merely popular to notorious.

On December 21, 1998, some thirty-odd celebrants were arrested by an overzealous Rudy Guiliani's clean, mean police machine.

We arrived at South Beach in Staten Island right on schedule—the bus was fine, traffic was okay—and proceeded down to the water line carrying special ritual bundles from the bus. Firewood. Drums. Flags. Cider. In no time at all, the fire teepee was constructed and we had cast our sacred circle around it. At precisely 8:56 pm, I lit the fire, and we began to drum and chant: "Reverence. Reverence. Reverence to Her."

We had been on the beach for only about fifteen minutes, when several cars loaded with cops arrived and told us to put out the fire and leave. Assuring them that we were there for ceremony and not for trouble, we did exactly as they told us to. We surrounded our solstice fire, carefully covered it with sand, and filed off the beach. But by the time we had all reached the parking lot, they wouldn't let us go.

Instead, they commandeered our bus, herded us inside, posted two armed officers to guard us, and drove us to the 122nd precinct, where, after hours of detention, we were given a summons to appear in court. It was only once we were released that we realized that several of our original participants had escaped at some point before we boarded the bus. As it turned out, they took advantage of their freedom to call the press, go on the Web, and in other ways try to establish an emergency support system for us.

This resulted in a full-blown media frenzy. The New York Post screamed, "33 Busted in Staten Island Cult Bash." A barrage of press followed, with stories appearing for weeks afterward in papers and on radio across the country. The New York Times championed our cause and published four major stories in four days, including a full-page feature about my Urban Shaman practice. The publicity led to the Civil Liberties Union taking our case. Both judges that we came in front of dropped the charges against us and released complimentary statements on our behalf that were published in law reviews across the country.

Now, thanks to the media and New York's Finest, the Winter Solstice, like the Spring Equinox, has entered popular culture and achieved the status of a mainstream holiday. This mass awareness of Earth-honoring, seasonal ceremonies only took thirty-five years to attain. So, the way I figure it is, I just have two more to go. All I have to do is boost public awareness and observance of the Fall Equinox and the Summer Solstice to the same mass audience and I will be able to retire, my job as an urban shaman complete!

Mama Donna Henes is an urban shaman, award-winning author, popular speaker, and workshop leader. She has published four books, a CD, and an acclaimed quarterly journal; she writes a column for UPI (United Press International) *Religion and Spirituality Forum. For the past thirty-five years, she has tracked and celebrated the cosmic cycles of the seasons, as well as the universal seasons of human life. Mama Donna's special concern is finding ways to reconnect the urban population with the wondrous workings of the natural world. To that end, she leads joyful celebrations of celestial events that have introduced ancient traditional rituals and contemporary ceremonies to millions of people in more than 100 cities since 1972. Mama Donna maintains a ceremonial center, spirit shop, and ritual practice; she consults with individuals, groups, institutions, municipalities, and corporations to create meaningful ceremonies for every imaginable occasion. Mama Donna Henes can be contracted through her Web site at http://www.thequeenofmyself.com/*

Illustrations: Lydia Hess

A City Witch Reflects on Life in the Country

Boudica

I grew up in New York City. When I found my path as a witch, during my late teens, it was easy to find much of what I needed for my practice in New York. But it was harder to find the connection to the Earth that is essential for an earth-based witch. Years later, after I traded city living for life in the country, the things that drew me to the country became the links I needed to make that essential connection. I also found, in some instances, that what had seemed important in the city had no real substance or deep value to me. I learned that the more things are different, the more they are the same, and sometimes we have to be careful what we wish for because we could end up with something we didn't expect. On the other hand, what we get can be exactly what we are looking for.

In this article, I compare my life as a witch in the city to my life as a witch in the country. I also share with you some differences in the treatment of the Wheel of the Year, similarities and differences in practices and, finally, I mention the diversity of the people in both places.

Seasons in the City

The seasons are the obvious indicators of change no matter where you go. Living in the northern hemisphere just south of New England, there are very distinct seasons. This holds true in Europe as well, where some northern countries experience a full range of seasons. But in urban areas, no matter where you are, the seasonal changes are subtle. The space allowed for nature is restricted to parks and outlying areas, and you need to know where to look to observe the change of season. (We had a tree in front of our house, and when it was not bare, it was either green or brown.)

In springtime, city dwellers must look quick or miss the budding leaves. An almost natural environment can be found in the parks that sprout green at the first sign of spring. Seasonal flowers may be found in the parks, too, but looking in stores is one of the best ways to track the seasons in the city. It's a little tricky because things will appear two to three months in advance of the season. The spring clothing lines come out in late fall, and winter clothing lines come out in summer. It's a sure sign summer is just about over when, in late June, the back-to-school fashions are in Bloomingdale's windows.

In the country, the changes of season are very clear. Spring is spring, and spring flowers appear all over the countryside. Fall is marked with market stands selling fresh produce and by the brown, red, and gold leaves and grasses of the season. It is also possible to see bushel baskets full of spring blooms and fresh, seasonal produce in city stores in the fall because exotic food stuffs are imported from warmer climates.

The solstices and equinoxes are easier to follow than the Wheel of the Year. Living in the country, you notice the lengthening and the shortening of the days, while in the city we lived in subways, tall buildings with few windows, and even if we were outdoors, we roamed the concrete city between the steel- and glass-mountains. It is much easier to listen to the weatherman on the evening news as he tells the exact time the seasons change. The best almanac I ever had was the local weather guy who provided all sorts of information about the seasonal changes, weather patterns, sky watch alerts, and old wives tales that most people regarded as in the "did you know" category, rather than taken seriously, as country folk do. I never missed a solstice or an equinox. We had weather maps instead of a book that explained the cycles of the Earth to us. I still use those tools to judge if I should water my tomatoes in the evening, or let nature do it; and to guide my decisions about whether to pick late-season veggies or cover them to protect them from frost so they can ripen another day or two. While I am not prone to working with tools all the time, they are great for ritual use, and they are valuable when they vary in cultural significance and are used to create a diverse environment for you or your group's practice.

In the city, I had an array of diverse cultures to choose from. Botanicas were abundant and with those stores came the exotic oils, herbs, and incenses made specifically for magical workings.

The seven candles were always great tools for special workings. Sometimes, the store owner would "share" a little secret or working when he or she recognized that someone was genuinely interested in the Craft. But it is possible to find specialty stores outside the city if you know where to look. I've found hoodoo shops and little bookstores in the strangest places. There is a wonderful little Chinese herbal shop in a city not too far away from me that has some novel little trinkets and supplies as well as great herbs. The same diversity is available in the country.

Whether cultural, sexual, spiritual, or political, the one thing that marks people who live within large urban areas is that they learn to live with diversity, or they leave.

Where we find tools is also interesting. In the city we had all those expensive specialty stores that sold made-to-order wands, capes, and so forth. (Louis Vuitton medicine bags anyone? Or how about Dolce & Gabbana ceremonial capes? Ohh! Jimmy Choo ceremonial sandals! Or, if you prefer classic, how about Chanel silver pentacles or oils for your workings?) Did you know that Chanel uses a patchouli base in its perfumes? That's probably why so many witches love the smell of Chanel.

There are also the weekend garage sales, where we could purchase someone's quaint leftovers, and those high-end auction houses that cater to dealers, not common folks. You still spend an arm and a leg for a stone crystal that should have cost you a couple of dollars. Out in the country, we have flea markets, and I've found $5 cauldrons, 25-cent occult books, cheap stones, and good fresh herbs. There are some great bargains to be had.

Oh, let us not forget cakes and ale. I have found some wonderful Amish cakes and reasonably priced ale at local wineries. While the selection isn't what you would find at a New York City "takeout fest" that can be found at some coven's open rituals, the country offers rich and earthy, down-home desserts and some of the best potlucks I've ever attended. There is something about fresh, homemade dishes that connects me to the earth, to the simple things that the Craft is supposed to be.

The acceptance factor is a very big issue with me, and it was one of the biggest drawbacks of my choice to move to the country. While I found no acceptance issues when I lived in New York City, it is a very different matter here in middle America. Within a city there is such diversity it is impossible to live there and not be caught up in the concept. Whether cultural, sexual, spiritual, or political, the one thing about people in large urban areas is that they learn to live with diversity, or they leave. Most of the people I encountered in the forty-plus years I lived there had learned to celebrate diversity and enjoy all the wonderful elements that go with it.

In addition to the wonderful assortment of food, clothing, language, art, music, and so much more, spirituality is expressed in the variety of churches, mosques, temples, and other markings or buildings that represent various spiritual paths or correspond to Deity in some manner. It is very different here in the country. While we enjoy the comforts of country life and work and shop amongst the local people, the fundamentalist movement is alive and well. I have taken to not discussing my beliefs with people until I get to know them, and they me. My symbols of faith are many times worn under my shirt, so I don't scare the locals. A Christian minister placed a binding spell on me on a local newspaper bulletin board in response to a thank-you I wrote for a positive article on the pagan headstones that they published. Go figure.

Do not get me wrong. We have met, talked with, and enjoyed the company of many pagans here in the country. But there is also

a lunatic fringe, and I am surprised their followers do not question what they say and allow these kinds of people to speak for them and to represent them. But, then again, we also have our own lunatic fringe pagan fundamentalists, which confirms that no matter what faith you are dealing with, you will find a few bad apples if you look in the right places.

I do miss the conversations. People here have very different concerns and interests from those I once had. And while I care about how the weather is affecting the crops and how bad the unemployment is, I do miss the discussions on politics, music, and art. I guess that's why I stick to my computer and why I have the *New York Times* bookmarked

and read it several times a week. I manage to kee~
witchy fashions and the latest and greatest book r~

This brings me to one more issue—the Int~
first year here, I had dial-up because cable or ~
Sorry, but I am a high-tech witch, and dial-up was n~
computer is an essential part of communication and a way to ~
supplies. Being able to shop for things online that are not available locally is something to consider if you ever move out to the country.
The search for a better Internet connection led to trying various types
of connections. Satellite was the only high-speed broadband connection for a while, but it is an expensive, inferior option compared to a
cable or a DSL connection. Fortunately, DSL has arrived, and the last
few months have been blissful.

There are benefits and drawbacks to both lifestyles. I may be a
country witch now, but I retain a very city flavor that stretches from
my job to my spiritual practice and my home. I hope you have enjoyed this little trip between lifestyles and next time you see me online, do tell me if there is a sale going on at the witch department at
Bloomingdale's and if I can buy it online.

Boudica *is reviews editor and co-owner of* The Wiccan/Pagan Times
and owner of The Zodiac Bistro, *both online publications. She is a High
Priestess with the Mystic Tradition Teaching Coven of Pennsylvania, Ohio,
New Jersey, New York, and Maryland and is a guest speaker at many local
and East Coast events. A former New Yorker, she now resides with her
husband and six cats in Ohio.*

Illustrations: Paul Hoffman

Flying Solo

James Kambos

The image of a village wise woman or wise man living in seclusion, tending gardens, and following the Old Religion has been a part of the Craft for centuries. As long as there have been practitioners of witchcraft, there have been solitary witches.

While many witches feel it is necessary to be part of a coven or group for spiritual growth and magickal work, and while working with a group certainly has many advantages, it can be rewarding, even exhilarating, to work alone. Being a solitary is as much a tradition as is being Dianic or Gardnerian.

Before I focus on both the positive and negative aspects of being a solitary practitioner, it's important to understand the role solitary witches have played in the history of the Craft and why many people follow this path.

Keeping the Faith Alive

During the dark era of the 1300s through the 1700s, when anti-witch hysteria swept through Europe and New England, witches and non-witches—Christians, Jews, gypsies, and pagans—were victimized. Needless to say, the coven as we know it today broke up. Their members scattered and became isolated. Written traditions and spells were either destroyed by witch-hunters or by witches themselves, because they feared for their own safety. Witches who were once members of nurturing covens found themselves practicing as solitaries. But these brave solitary witches didn't let the

> **In times of crisis the coven will come together to aid a member going through a rough period. . . . The solitary practitioner doesn't have this safety net.**

Craft die. In secrecy, they worshipped the old gods alone and, occasionally, they would pass their magickal wisdom on to a private pupil or family member. It wouldn't be until the mid-twentieth century that covens would begin to enjoy a renaissance. By this time solitary witchcraft had become an acceptable alternative to the conventional framework of a coven.

Why Practice Alone?

Belonging to a coven can be an enlightening, enjoyable experience and a good way to receive support from like-minded individuals. So

why would anyone want to be a solitary? The reasons are many, but let me make it clear that belonging to a coven or being a solitary is a matter of personal choice. Neither path is better than the other, and both have their positive and negative aspects. Also, neither choice needs to be permanent. As you go through different phases of your life, your spiritual needs can change. You may first be initiated into a coven and then feel a desire to pursue a solitary direction. Or, after studying about Wicca on your own, you may wish to experience the more formal structure of a coven at some point. It's up to you.

When a coven works together toward a specific magickal goal, the energy created can be immense. This doesn't mean, however, that a solitary can't create enough power to get the job done.

Many witches practice as a solitary because they have no other choice. Here's one such case. A Llewellyn reader once wrote me to ask for advice on being a solitary. This person lived in a small conservative town and came from a family of devout Christians who wouldn't understand the pagan lifestyle. Sometimes, the only support a solitary can find comes from books or Internet sites. Other individuals are so free and independent that being a solitary simply fits their lifestyle. Whatever the reason, a solitary witch of the twenty-first century can live an urban, suburban, or rural lifestyle and work in the cubicle next to you, or be the soccer mom next door.

Deciding if Being Solitary is Right for You

Coven? Or solitary? Neither system is perfect, and neither can meet all of your needs at all times. Let's take a practical look at the pros and cons of each path, as they pertain to certain key issues.

Emotional Support

In times of crisis the coven will come together to aid a member going through a rough period. For example, if the coven member has thoughts of using negative magick to get back at someone, the group can help calm the member. Positive solutions can be discussed and carried out. The solitary practitioner doesn't have this safety net. They must rely on their own inner strength and seek guidance from meditation, dream work, and affirmations. On the upside, this can be a time of helpful self-evaluation.

Raising Power

When a coven works together toward a specific magickal goal, the energy created can be immense. This doesn't mean, however, that a solitary can't create enough power to get the job done. While the power of the group may work more quickly, the power of the solitary will be more focused. A solitary works for his or her own need and can focus all of their power into their goal. The group may raise more power more quickly, but everyone must be on the same wavelength. Within the magick circle, the coven can raise a larger cone of power, but the smaller cone of power created by the solitary will be just as effective.

Rituals

Most covens have a set format for ceremonies. This can be a moving experience, or it can become too scripted. The solitary has the freedom to introduce something new and spontaneous if the time feels right without stepping on someone's toes. Other advantages the lone practitioner has are that the words of a ritual or chant can be kept to a minimum, the ritual tools will have a more personal feel to them than those belonging to a group, and only the tools they feel comfortable using need to be selected.

When to Meet

Deciding when to have a coven meeting or service can sometimes be a hassle. It can even be hard to get people together to observe a sabbat; and if there is an emergency, it can be a major undertaking to contact everyone. The solitary needs only to decide for himself or herself when and how to observe a sabbat or perform a major ritual. And if a problem should arise that needs magickal work, the solitary can start on it quickly without having to contact anyone else.

Specialized Talents

In a magickal group, members will be skilled in different areas. Someone may be proficient with the tarot or runes. Another may have psychic abilities, and someone else might have musical talent. Naturally, the solitary can only draw upon his or her own areas of expertise. To make up for

A core belief of witchcraft is that free will and personal choice should be respected.

this drawback, a solitary could join forces occasionally with another magickal person who has different strengths.

Relationships

The bonds formed between coven members can be as strong as the bonds we feel with our families. In many instances, coven members become closer than family. There's also the flip side. We've all heard (or experienced) the horror stories about dealing with a know-it-all coven member or members with an attitude. Solitaries don't need to deal with those issues. True, they'll miss out on the positive social aspects of a coven, but some people just function better alone. It might be difficult for some to understand, but it can be genuinely uplifting to practice the Craft alone. It's your faith, your magick, your way!

A Word About Self-Initiation

I can hear some of you saying, "No way!" First of all, many solitaries were probably initiated into a coven at some point in the past, and that's fine.

But there is no reason why someone who is serious about the craft, adheres to the Craft's basic beliefs, and follows the witches' Creed, can't initiate themselves as a witch.

I don't have the space here to go into details about specific self-initiation rituals. My only suggestion is that the initiation be performed on a sabbat or from the New to Full Moon. And it may be as simple or complex as you wish.

If anyone questions you about the validity of self-initiation, ask them the age-old question: Who initiated the first witch?

A core belief of witchcraft is that free will and personal choice should be respected. As you consider different paths, think about why you were drawn to the craft in the first place. Take time to write your own list about what you like and dislike about group/solitary work. Meditate on your list and listen to your inner voice. Let your free will guide you to the path of your choice.

Resources

Buckland, Raymond. *Buckland's Complete Book of Witchcraft*. Originally published in 1986. St. Paul, MN: Llewellyn, 1988.

Valiente, Doreen. *Witchcraft for Tomorrow*. Originally published in 1978. Custer, WA: Phoenix Publishing, 1987.

Weinstein, Marion. *Positive Magic*. Originally published in 1978. Custer, WA: Phoenix Publishing, 1981.

James Kambos *is a solitary who lives in Appalachia. He enjoys crafting spells based on the magickal traditions of his Greek ancestors, and discovering the folk magick ways of rural Appalachia where he was raised. His pastimes include raising herbs and vegetables, and cooking.*

Illustrations: Rik Olson

Witchcraft Essentials

Practices, Rituals & Spells

Living as a Tantrik Witch

Chandra Alexandre

In 1998, I was in a small seaside
town in India that is renowned as
a pilgrimage site for the Lord of the
universe. I had gone there to explore
my spiritual inclinations and decide if
committing to Devi, the Goddess, was
right to do. As a witch, I was in a quan-
dary about my spiritual beliefs and the
implications of my actions. If I accepted Hinduism and a Hindu goddess,
could I still practice the Craft? Could I
pledge myself to Goddess Kali and still
find community back home? Could I
be a witch and a Hindu? How would
I worship? And what of Sanskrit, that

challenging and ancient language of the gods I would have to be-friend? Those and many other questions swam in my head in the craziness of the subcontinent's summer heat. Then, when it seemed I could think no longer and must make a decision, I was given the answer in the form of a date. The auspicious night for initiation was determined by astrological means to be August 2. With this, the cloud of doubt and uncertainty that had been hanging over me lifted, and I knew it would be all right. She was telling me, with this Lammas invitation offered in the middle of a temple at her lotus feet, I could be a witch and a Hindu. She could, and would, have me both ways.

Upon returning from India with a yearning in my heart to share what I had learned, I was surprised to find few resources to support the modern witch who, like me, wanted to explore connection to the ancient, living spiritual tra-ditions of Hindu India. While looking to be with others in the creation of meaningful worship and hoping to create a public forum in which practitioners of all varieties and levels could gather and enjoy ritual, I began  practicing a syncretism of faith I call Sha'can (a coming together of Shakta for a goddess-worshipping Hindu and Wiccan for a goddess-worshiping westerner). With this, SHARANYA was born.

SHARANYA is a modern goddess temple dedicated in service through the Sha'can tradition to the creation of safe spaces for wor-ship, devotion, and learning. Ours is a community for those who love the essentials of Hindu thought and the spiritual technologies of tantra and who seek to explore and experience these systems while not diminishing the beauty or truth of an existing earth-based spirituality. We offer an open welcome to all who wish to approach goddesses such as Kali and Durga, but might be afraid to do so for lack of knowledge, a qualified teacher, or fear of cultural appropriation. We're here for individuals who are curious about tantric ceremonial practices or wonder how to invite Shiva (lord of the cosmic dance) or Sarasvati (goddess of learning and the arts) and fully experience the essence of that deity rather than to utilize a Hindu deity within a pagan ceremony.

With this as background, I offer here some of the introductory teachings shared through the Daughters of Kali, our gender-inclusive year-and-a-day working circle. Specifically, this is an unveiling of two important practices from the Indian subcontinent that anyone can incorporate into an existing system of worship and use to enhance ritual work and psycho-spiritual development. It comes with an assurance that strengthening your spiritual core does not depend upon the language you speak, the way you worship, or that the method used is derived from an ancient Indian tradition—a tradition about which you may know virtually nothing when you begin. Much, out of necessity, is left up to you to explore. Beyond that, it is left up to faith and a belief in the power of the work itself to generate meaning. How far you take it, and how deep you go, is up to you. From these basic practices, much may be revealed.

An Overview of Tantra

Myriad gods and goddesses—from Ganesha, the ever-popular elephant-headed deity, to Kali, the sometimes frightening yet ever-compassionate mother—offer refuge, blessings, and the necessary challenges to those seeking them. Fortunately, they do so with a blind eye toward country of birth and religious orientation. Tantra,

similarly, welcomes everyone. A branch of Hinduism that incorporates both indigenous and scripture-based wisdom, tantra is an ancient spiritual system that weaves together the worlds of humanity and the Divine. It seeks, ultimately, a return to the Source of all creation through direct engagement with both the Great Mystery and the more mundane aspects of living. For tantriks, all of life is deemed worthy of attention, because we learn something about the fundamental nature of reality through life's variety. Some say that the Source, when we wish to understand it, is female; and some say it's male. Regardless, most tantriks agree that it is the yearning of the Divine for itself that facilitates the involution of spirit into matter and, hence, the manifestation of the world as we know it.

Studying tantra is a fast track toward enlightenment. Why? Because as a tantrik, we must be willing to ride the edge of our deepest fears. Anyone willing and able to do that can experience the soul freed from the limitations of fear. However, this is no easy task. It is a task that requires commitment, focus, devotion, and a good guide on the path. It requires the kind of unwavering strength of purpose that is only gained through willingness to overcome all illusions, including those stemming from religious, cultural, familial, or societal dictates (either internal or external).

For the witch, tantra offers potential for both deep insight into, and practical assistance with, the basics of living a spiritual life. This is true because both paths share a belief in the importance of this phenomenal world, reverence for nature, respect for the interrelationship between self and cosmos, and a willingness to alter consciousness for the purpose of achieving desired ends (in alignment with moral and ethical guidelines, of course). Tantra provides tools for everyday living as much as it does for circle work, with things such as grounding, centering, raising energy, and creating sacred space that are central to its philosophy on how to get closer to the God and Goddess.

Sadhana is spiritual practice, and without pranayama (breath work) and dhyana (meditation), nothing is accomplished.

Through vehicles such as breath work, chanting, meditation, *japa* (repetition of divine names), sacred diagrams, hand gestures, and ritual, tantra offers the spiritual aspirant methods of strengthening their spiritual self in preparation for the truly difficult task of surrendering to the Divine.

It is no secret that many of the fundamentals of Wicca are derived or adapted from Hindu tantra. Examples include how we cast a circle, invoke the directions, purify the space, place importance on the elements (earth, air, fire, water, and ether), and draw down the deity to be worshipped. But the true grace of tantra is its scientific understanding of energy and its utilization of the life force in the creation of conscious connection to self and spirit. This is absolutely essential to effective spellwork, not to mention the development of other spiritual powers such as lucid dreaming, shamanic journeying, and hands-on healing. Here, then, is an introduction to traditional tantrik techniques made accessible and relevant to the Western condition and our pagan religiosity. Practice them diligently, and you too will be on the path of the tantrik witch.

Spiritual Technologies

I am frequently asked what the most important elements of *sadhana* are. *Sadhana* is spiritual practice, and without *pranayama* (breath work) and *dhyana* (meditation), nothing is accomplished. Both of these spiritual technologies are essential to the spiritual seeker, be she tantrik or witch. These are foundational practices capable of aiding both the neophyte and the more accomplished practitioner, whether doing solitary or group work.

Pranayama

Prana means "life-force energy." *Pranayama* is the path of practice that recognizes and seeks to hone that life-force energy. In tantra, this energy is *prana-shakti*, the female force, and is understood to be carried on and moved through the breath. Of course, everyone alive breathes. Consciously or (usually) unconsciously, we are kept alive by an inflow and outflow of air, our lungs facilitating the exchange of nutrients and waste in a cycle that sustains and interconnects. Making breath conscious is the first and most fundamental lesson

of pranayama, the first step toward a tantrik practice. How do we do this?

First, sit comfortably on the floor or in a chair, or lie down. Begin by placing your right hand on your heart and your left hand on your belly (just below the belly button). This facilitates the flow of energy in the body in a balanced and gentle way.

Now close your eyes and bring your focus to the point between your eyebrows. This is the *ajna chakra* (the third eye). It is the energy center associated with the quality of balance, harmony between masculine and feminine energies, and the faculties of union and insight. It is the coming together of Sun, Moon, and fire—a place of movement toward mind-body-spirit harmony.

Allow your mind to relax as your body relaxes, and begin to draw your awareness to your breath. As you strengthen your focus, remain relaxed throughout your body. You want to be able to take full, deep breaths from the bottom of your belly to the very top of your lungs, imagining your breath flowing like a wave on your inhalation from your belly, through your diaphragm and lungs, and almost up to your throat. On your exhalation, release the wave slowly, gradually sending the air out in the reverse pattern, drawing in your belly in the final stages to ensure that all the air has been completely expelled.

Again, try to stay focused only on the breath, breathing comfortably as you do so. Practice this until you can retain your focus and your mind does not wander. You will begin to discern greater awareness and clarity after each exercise. Once you feel comfortable with this pranayama practice, you may wish to deepen it by retaining your breath at the beginning and end of each wave, allowing for a space of rest, silence, and peacefulness to be held after each inhalation and exhalation. Feel into the present moment of each breath, and with this, begin to cultivate the benefits of pranayama.

This spiritual technology is the foundation of all others. As a witch, you will quickly come to understand the ways this practice can aid you—for example, by increasing the amount of energy to which you have access, by facilitating your ability to work with the energies of the subtle body, by making it easier for you to ground and center; and, by guiding you into the realm of the internal energy channels where even deeper work and spiritual transformation can occur.

MEDITATION

From pranayama, it is easy to proceed right into meditation and, in fact, one usually precedes the other. Tantrik meditation, known as *dhyana* in Sanskrit, is different from meditation in other traditions in that it is a process of focusing rather than of release. The goal of meditation is to cultivate awareness of what lies at the innermost recesses of consciousness, allowing the *sadhaka* (practitioner) to move beyond ego and desire for power, eventually beyond time itself, into a realm where the essential self and the building blocks of creation may be found. Meditation is a powerful tool that further develops spiritual-core strength, deepens connection to the Divine, and, over time, helps practitioners open to an abundance of energy called *kundalini shakti*, with which it is possible to further spiritual aims.

There are many ways to begin meditation. In tantra, a primary vehicle for developing adeptness with focus, as well as with movement beyond the limitations of the individual sense of "I-am," is to utilize a *bija mantra*. A hallmark of tantrik practice, a bija mantra is a one-syllable sound that stems from and connects together the origins of cosmic creation. These bija or "seed" mantras all spread out from the original sound, A*um* (A = creation; U = preservation; M = dissolution), which is followed by the silence of potentiality in a never-ending cycle of birth, life, death, and rebirth. By uttering a bija mantra such as Aum, one invites into alignment through vibration the gross (physical), subtle (psychical), and causal bodies (etheric); thus, bringing together the microcosm of the individual and the macrocosm of the universal. Furthermore, like a seed, a bija contains within itself the potential for growth and transformation, and this potential may be activated through dedicated recitation, creating within the practitioner a strong foundation from which realizations of essence, or soul, may be uncovered.

Bija also means "drop," and *mantra* is sacred sound—that which tunes the mind's awareness. At the core, a bija mantra is a drop of the ocean of consciousness, which, in turn, is the vibrational energy of existence. Like a hologram, the bija mantra contains within it not only a unique identity, but also an expression of the entire ocean from which it comes. Created from the fifty-one letters of the Sanskrit alphabet, each bija is connected to every other bija through relationships of sound, as well as to all other possibilities of sound manifestation. The entire alphabet is given the name *varna mala*, or garland of letters, for this reason.

To begin your sadhana (spiritual practice), find a quiet place and sit comfortably in a spot especially chosen for this work. Make sure that your spine is straight, as it serves as a conduit of energy between your root connection and your crown opening to the sky. As in pranayama, allow your focus to come to your breath and then bring your internal gaze softly into focus at your third eye. From here, set your intention, creating a *sankalpa* (sacred purpose) for the practice. Now, as you are comfortable, begin to drop your focus to your heart center and breathe from there, imagining a pink-colored lotus flower opening a little bit more with each breath. The heart is a key energy center in meditation, serving as a gateway between the qualities of the phenomenological world and the expanse of that which lies outside of, or transcends it. The pink color symbolizes the coming together of male and female qualities in a union that goes beyond the limitations of the mundane realm and into the possibilities for an alchemical sacred marriage.

Once the flower is completely open, begin reciting your chosen bija mantra. There are many from which to choose, for example:

RAM (ruh-m) for Agni, god of fire; GAM (guh-m) for Ganesha, remover of obstacles; LAM (luh-m) for the *muladhara chakra* (root chakra), or energy of earth; HRAUM (huh-roum) for Shiva, god of dissolution; HRIM (huh-reem) for Durga, the inaccessible goddess; and KRIM (kreem) for

Kali, goddess of time, she who takes away darkness. The mantra is to be spoken out loud at first, slowly pronouncing the syllable and bringing increasing focus to each utterance (as you recite, do not move your tongue from its first placement; and for Kali's bija, do not close your lips to say the "M" as you repeat it—Sanskrit flows when pronounced properly—and this bija will sound like KRING when recited repeatedly). Gradually gain speed in your recitation, allowing the mantra to turn over and over in your mouth, with the reverberations of sound echoing throughout your body. These, you will find, have healing properties. Then, when you feel the time is right, slowly soften your speech to a whisper and gradually bring the mantra inside. You will be reciting your chosen mantra with your mind alone. Do not waver in your focus. Allow the sound to create a solid internal foundation. Develop this core strength, and you will make a place from which all other spiritual exercises may be initiated.

Over time, you will be able to go further with both these practices, cultivating greater awareness and fortitude through constancy and diligence. Take your time in developing this strength, gifting yourself with a dedicated practice of at least five minutes of pranayama and meditation a day. Certainly, do more if you are able; but do not let an overcommitment keep you from doing your spiritual homework! If all you can manage reliably is five minutes a day, then by all means, know that it will greatly benefit you to do just that.

Chandra Alexandre is the founder and executive director of SHARAN-YA, The Maa Batakali Cultural Mission, Inc., and the originator of its Sha'can tradition. She teaches and lives by principles of deep ecumenism, belief in the importance of open-source religion, and a commitment to engaged spirituality. Chandra has traveled to India for over ten years on pilgrimage, and she honors her maternal grandmother as her first spiritual teacher. She received diksha (initiation) from Shyam Sundar Dash, a

Knots, Beads, and Strings: Pagan Prayer Beads

Susan Pesznecker

Have you noticed some of your fellow witches handling strings of beads during spellwork or ritual? What are coming to be known as "pagan prayer beads" or "pagan rosaries" first came into use in India as the traditional Hindu *mala*, strings of 108 identical beads made from the seeds of sacred plants. Malas were used as a focus for chanting or meditating. Buddhists borrowed the bead strings from their own use, and the beads gradually spread through religious groups in Europe and Asia. While their best-known use is via Catholicism's holy rosary, today's witches and pagans have also adopted prayer

beads for their own use. Beautiful to use and satisfying to make, the beads are a meaningful addition to one's spiritual and magickal practices.

Pagan bead strings differ from traditional malas or rosaries in two key ways. First, malas and rosaries typically use set numbers of identical beads, with perhaps one or two different "marker beads" within the string. In contrast, pagan bead strings contain a variety of patterns, colors, and numbers of beads, as well as charms, pendants, and other additions. Second, malas and rosaries follow traditional, identical patterns, while pagan bead strings are as different and unique as the people who make them.

Designing a Bead String

Begin by considering why you're making the string. Perhaps you will use it for prayer, meditation, or ritual. The string might encode personal symbolism, track your mastery of a course of study, or mark passage or initiation. You could use the beads as a talisman, anchoring or capturing a magickal essence. You might even match the string to a favorite chant, poem, or blessing. The possibilities are endless. Think, too, about how you'll use the string. Will you wear it? Hold it? Use it on your altar space or as a magickal decoration? Will you complete the string in one sitting or continue to add to it over time?

As your plan takes shape, consider the materials. Will you use plastic beads? Metal? Wood? Stone? Will you favor identical beads, or do you have any special items or charms to incorporate? What about colors, textures, or numbers? You may wish to consider magickal or elemental correspondences: an earthy-witch might choose to work in beads of wood or green agate, while a watery-pagan might use blue glass beads and shells. Visit your local bead store for ideas.

Ask yourself what sort of string you'll use? Hemp? Cording? Yarn? Wire? Your choice of material will be related to the beads you select. Your approach can be as simple as stringing beads on a leather cord and knotting the ends or as complex as working with silver wire and jeweler's tools. If you take the simpler approach, consider the knots you'll use: they all have their own magickal symbolism.

The **square knot** is useful for tying two separate, same-sized strings together securely. The four-sided knot symbolizes joining, balance, the four quarters, elements, or directions. When tying, remember, "right over left, left over right."

The **overhand knot** (you know this as the starter knot in tying one's shoelaces) is a simple stopper knot. It ties a "stop" at the end of a cord or a "spacer" between beads. The apparent division of the knot into a "triskele" of three parts makes it a good choice for magick referencing a trinity.

The **figure-eight knot** is another kind of stopper knot. Tied loosely, it resembles the infinity symbol and makes an elegant design. The knot symbolizes the idea of eternity, cycles, or connectivity. It makes an excellent stopper between knots or an attractive spacer between beads.

The **bowline** (BOH-linn) knot is used to create a permanent, nonslipping loop on a rope. In a bead string, you can use a bowline to set a "circle" from which might dangle an amulet, talisman, or a special bead. When tying, remember: "the bunny comes out of the hole, goes around the tree, and dives back into the hole."

The knots used in your prayer strings may be functional, decorative, or both. Use different colors or textures and combine or braid strands for special effects.

When you're ready to create the actual design, use paper and pencil to sketch the design and/or pattern to scale. This method suits those who prefer symmetry and structural uniformity. Alternatively, just open yourself to inspiration and start stringing, trusting that your inner magickal self will shape the results. Always use a piece of string that's two to four times longer than you think you'll need, allowing for length taken up by knots and large beads.

If you plan to handle your beads as a prayer or meditative tool, adding small spacer beads between each main bead makes the larger beads easier to grasp and "work." Small metal beads, or colored seed beads, are often used as spacers. If using small beads, work with wire or very thin cord, and use a long beading needle.

Making Beads

Thanks to craft stores, it's easy to purchase beads of all shapes, sizes, and materials. But it's also fun and reasonably simple to craft your own. Paper beads are inexpensive and quick to make. Wrap elongated equilateral triangles (1 to 2 inches wide and 3 to 4 inches long) of thin paper around a round toothpick, starting with the wide end. Add periodic dabs of white glue to strengthen the bead as you wrap, but be careful not to glue the bead to the stick. Brush the finished bead with diluted white glue and allow it to dry on the toothpick. Use colored, patterned, or metallic paper for varied results.

Other ideas: Small pieces of wood or dried seeds can be made interesting beads by using a hobby drill or a "gimlet" tool to drill holes in them; use clay like FIMO or Sculpey (which are baked) to create beads of varied sizes, shapes, and colors; or create "metal" beads by rolling bits of foil around a toothpick. Seal with clean nail polish.

Ideas for Sample Bead Strings

Four Elements String

Use even numbers of beads in the four elemental colors and separate each section with a larger metal charm or a special bead for the solstices and equinoxes. Include natural materials, and use square

knots. Use the beads as an altar decoration or work with them when doing a seasonal ritual.

PRAYER OR CHANT STRING

Create a bead string that follows a favorite chant, reading, or prayer. Use colors and materials that compliment your intention. As you repeat or sing the chant, hold the string in your hands and "tick off" the beads as you complete each line, stanza, and so on.

LUNAR STRING

Use silver wire and beads in blue, white, and silver to create thirteen segments, one for each annual lunar cycle. Separate each lunation with a crystal "Moon" bead and include figure-eight knots in the string. Use the beads in lunar ritual or wrap around a moon-oriented wand or stave.

PATRON STRING

Choose colors, patterns, and charms that appeal to or honor your chosen patron or deity. Use a bowline knot to dangle a special bead or token that symbolizes the patron.

ACCOMPLISHMENT STRING

Create a string that encodes a magickal discipline or course of study. This string will evolve and change over time, becoming a visual record of your progress. Make it long enough to wear with magickal garb.

Your bead string will be a colorful and valuable addition to your magickal kit. Enjoy!

Resources

Greer, John Michael and Clare Vaughn. *Pagan Prayer Beads*. San Francisco: Weiser, 2007.

Wiley, Eleanor. A *String and a Prayer: How to Make and Use Prayer Beads*. San Francisco: Weiser, 2002.

Susan "Moonwriter" Pesznecker *has practiced earth-based spirituality for two and a half decades. After twenty-five years as a nurse, she went back to school, earned a master's degree in nonfiction writing, and switched professions, becoming a college English teacher. Sue has published several nonfiction essays and the book* Gargoyles *(Career Press, 2007) and* Crafting Magick with Pen and Ink *(Llewellyn, 2009). Sue teaches magick online at the Grey School of Wizardry and is preparing to open the Earthkeepers School of Green Magick, which will focus on nature-based magick and ethical earth-keeping. She lives in beautiful northwest Oregon and enjoys herbology, organic gardening, writing, exploring the outdoors, and working magick.*

Illustrations: Neil Brigham

Crafting the Perfect Spell

Deborah Blake

Almost all witches use magick in one form or another, and almost everyone who practices magick will eventually cast a spell. Spells are written or spoken words, often accompanied by actions and equipment of some sort that are intended to bring about a specific result. You could think of them as tools. Specifically, power tools that are energized by our Will rather than by electricity.

Like regular tools, spells are only as good as the skills of those who wield them, and if used incorrectly, spells can even backfire and cause unintended harm. And like regular tools, the better the quality of the spell, the better the end result you are likely to achieve.

There are many books, some of them quite good, that contain spells for almost anything you might want, and there are times when using a spell out of a book is just fine. But if you have a truly important piece of magick to work, I strongly suggest you write your own spell.

There are a couple of reasons for this. To begin with, you know what you are trying to accomplish better than anyone else. For instance, a prosperity spell out of a book might work well under most circumstances, but if you are trying to find a new job that will allow you to stay home with your child while still advancing your career, you might need to come up with something much more specific.

In addition, the more of your energy you put into any given part of a spell, the more power you give it. So, in the case of the theoretical spell above, if you are using a green candle and some basil, the spell will be more forceful if you grew the herbs, made the candle, and then anointed it with homemade prosperity oil. Now, most of us aren't going to do all those steps every time (although I do recommend growing your own herbs when you can), but we can all write our own spells. Even if you don't think of yourself as a writer, you can craft your own perfect spell once you learn a few important essentials of spellcasting.

To Cast or not to Cast, that is the Question

The first essential element of spellcasting is deciding whether or not to use a spell at all. After all, you don't always need a power tool. Some jobs are just as easily done with a simple screwdriver. So, before you get started, you need to decide if a spell is really the right tool to deal with the problem at hand. Take a long, honest look at the situation, and see which one of these categories fits the best.

WHEN *TO* CAST A SPELL

- When you have exhausted all the mundane options but still need to achieve a goal (the spell not only puts your intention out into the universe, but is also a way of asking for help)

- When the spell will affect only you (such as casting a spell to open yourself to love)

- When you know what you want and are willing to do the work required to get it (like putting in applications at appropriate places after asking for the perfect job)

- When only good can come from the spell

WHEN *NOT TO* CAST A SPELL

- When there is a simple solution that doesn't require magick (you need to lose five pounds, haven't tried a diet yet, and have plenty of time)

- When casting a spell would interfere with someone's free will (casting a love spell to get a particular person, for instance)

- When you aren't sure what you really want to achieve (if you are uncertain of the end results you want, it is hard to truly focus enough *will* to make a spell work)

- When there is the possibility of causing harm to yourself or to others (remember: Harm None!)

If you are certain that the best solution for the situation is casting a spell, then it is time to get down to work and craft yourself the perfect spell to get the job done.

Ingredients for the Perfect Spell

The next essential element of spellcasting is to decide on your magickal goal. It is a good idea to write this down, unless it is very simple, and get as specific as possible. One of the trickiest parts of spellcasting is the balance between being as specific as you can (so you are intensely focused on the purpose of your spell) while leaving an opening for the gods to grant your request in ways that you might not have considered (since in my experience, this is the way things happen more often than not).

If you are looking for that perfect job, you might want to specify that you want something that allows you to spend more time with your child, but don't say, "I want to work out of my house," in case there is an option that would allow you to work elsewhere but still have your child with you. See what I mean?

Once you have your goal set, you can gather a few additional tools to boost the spell. I like Elizabeth Barrette's explanation in her book *Composing Magic* for why we use "extras" when casting a spell. She says: "Most spells combine words, actions, and objects to create a kind of 'handle' for the Will to grasp, rather like using a wrench to tighten or loosen a nut that wouldn't yield to fingers alone." In other words, the addition of specific items and actions can help to rev up our magickal engines, giving us even more power for the spell than we would get from using words alone.

This is because the addition of each extra element helps us to focus just a little bit more by reinforcing our intention to create a magickal result. So, if you look for items that match the goal you

have set, you will be adding another layer of intent to the energy you put out into the universe with your words.

How you choose the additional items is up to you. Some people look in books for spell correspondences—colors, Moon phases, days of the week, herbs, oils, and more—that are often used for a specific task. For instance, when doing prosperity magick, many people use the color green, work their magick on a Thursday, use basil or peppermint, and maybe a piece of malachite or jade. On the other hand, there are many folks who simply use whatever items feel *right* to them. It is more a matter of style than anything else, and you can use whichever approach you prefer.

And sometimes you just have to make do with whatever you have on hand. If a spell needs to be done right away, and you only have a white candle, by all means use that and it will be fine. Remember that your will and your intent are what truly matter here.

So let's say you have your goal, and you've done your research and figured out which additional items you want to use. Now you need to write your spell. **Don't panic. You can do this.**

Writing the Perfect Spell

When you set out to write a spell, you need to decide a few things first. Are you going to call on a particular god and/or goddess? Are you going to use rhyme or not? Will you write something short that you can memorize or something longer that you will read off a piece of paper? Keep in mind that there is no "right" way to create a spell; it is all simply a matter of what will work best for you.

Many people like to call on the god and/or goddess who is most associated with a particular goal, especially if there is one in the pantheon they usually use. A witch who follows a primarily Celtic path might use Brigid for creativity, where another witch might call on the Greek Apollo. Or you can just address the spell to "god and goddess" or "powers of the universe."

. . . don't forget about the most important aspect of spellcasting—your will. Many witches do something specific to help them gather focus as they prepare to work magick.

You don't have to call on anyone or anything, of course, but I like to personalize most spells a bit. I often say, "Great Goddess, Great

God, please hear my plea" at the beginning of a spell, but again, this is a matter of personal taste. My suggestion, especially when you are starting to write spells, is to stick with whatever you usually use.

Which brings us to the issue of rhyming. It is traditional to have spells rhyme; it is said to give them more power. Who said this, and whether or not it is true, I couldn't say. That's tradition for you. But I can tell you that I prefer, most of the time, to have my spells rhyme. Sometimes just every other line, but rhyming adds rhythm and a sense of formality to a spell, and that can also help to focus your will. On the other hand, if rhyming makes you uncomfortable and you spend most of your time struggling to find something that rhymes with "checkbook," then by all means, don't bother. In the end, it is better to be at ease with what you're saying than it is to follow tradition, don't you think?

As for whether to memorize it or write it down, I don't believe it makes any difference. I usually write mine down and then read them out loud, because I want to make sure I get the words right, and my memory is lousy. But I have one or two spells I have used so often that I have them memorized, and I do like the freedom of being able to recite them any time, any place, even if I don't happen to have the original piece of paper with me.

The most important aspect of writing a spell is to choose your words carefully. No matter which god you call on or how beautiful your rhyme scheme, if you mean to ask for "the perfect man for me" and actually asked for "a good man"—and end up with some guy named Goodman, you're going to wish you'd spent a little more time picking the right words.

This is where the goal you wrote down earlier comes in handy. Look at what you are trying to attain, and make sure that this is what you are actually asking for. Some goals can be tricky. For instance, I've known people who asked for "abundance" and got an abundance of ants—seriously! So if what you want is enough money to pay your bills without worry, ask for that, don't just ask for "money."

And try to be careful to avoid accidentally interfering with free will or causing harm. When I do spells, I often add a line that includes the words, "for the good of all and according to the free will of all," or "in positive ways," just to be on the safe side.

Casting the Perfect Spell

All these ingredients add up to a pretty good spell: deciding on the specifics of your goal, gathering the additional elements needed to cast the spell, choosing who you will call upon for help, and picking out the perfect words to express your desire. If you want to take it a step further, you can also throw in some actions to reinforce your words, like burning a piece of paper with something you want to be rid of written on it.

But don't forget about the most important aspect of spellcasting—your *will*. Many witches do something specific to help them gather focus as they prepare to work magick. Some meditate, drum, chant, or burn sage. For others, the acts involved in creating their ritual, such as the casting of the circle and the lighting of candles, serve to send them on their journey from the mundane world into the more intense and focused magickal one.

Whichever path you take, the combination of your carefully chosen words and your strong and focused will can create a power tool of magick that you can use to achieve your heart's desire. The perfect spell is crafted from your own energy, put out into the universe in the form of words you wrote yourself. Try it, and see what a difference it can make.

RESOURCES

Barrette, Elizabeth. *Composing Magic: How to Create Magical Spells, Rituals, Blessings, Chants, and Prayers.* Franklin Lakes: New Page. 2007.

Deborah Blake *is a Wiccan high priestess who has been leading her current group, Blue Moon Circle, for four years. She is the author of* Goddess is in the Details *(Llewellyn, 2009),* Circle, Coven & Grove: A Year of Magickal Practice *(Llewellyn, 2007) and* Everyday Witch A to Z: An Amusing, Inspiring & Informative Guide to the Wonderful World of Witchcraft *(Llewellyn, 2008). Deborah was also a finalist in the Pagan Fiction Award Contest and her short story, "Dead and (Mostly) Gone," can be found in the* Pagan Fiction Anthology *(Llewellyn, 2008). When not writing, Deborah runs* The Artisans' Guild, *a cooperative shop she founded with a friend. She is also a jewelry maker, tarot reader, an ordained minister, and an intuitive energy healer. She lives in a 100-year-old farmhouse in rural upstate New York with five cats who supervise all her activities, both magickal and mundane.*

Ilustrations: Paul Hoffman

What Do You Hear? Music and Your Personal Practice

Jenett Silver

I hear my alarm and the cat meowing in my ear. There are birds outside, and the wind or rain. At work in a high school library, I hear keys tapping, doors opening and closing, and endless conversations. I come home and listen to music to help get me in the mood for my evening. I might sing or play my harp. And as I fall asleep, I often hear the cat purring next to me. All these sounds are a part of my day.

Over time, I've found ways to use sound in my personal practice, which helps me stay grounded in what matters most to me. One week, I may use a sound trigger to focus on a particular goal. The next week, I use a playlist to cope better with a chaotic time at work. I may make music for the sheer joy of it, or be inspired to write a chant for an upcoming ritual. Pick the tools that make sense for you, right now.

Sound all around Us

We can use sound in our daily lives as a key to focus our attention. Each time we hear that sound, we bring our attention back to our goal or focus. Perhaps your workplace is busy and noisy. Pick something you hear every hour or so. It might be the sound of the phone, a particular person's voice, or a chime on your computer. Each time

you hear that sound, pause, take a deep breath, and focus on your goal today at your job. That's a trigger.

You can use this with any goal: each time you hear the trigger, repeat your goal to yourself. The more regularly you use it, the better it works: your brain will hear that sound, and automatically begin to relax and focus on something good. This not only gets you closer to your goals but it will help reduce your stress and frustration.

Expand this idea to learn more about the world around you. Take those birds outside my window. I hear them and might choose to learn more about what birds they are and what species live in my area. I could find ways to encourage birds near my home. Those decisions would mean learning more about the world around me and connecting with it in a new way, and each one started because I paid attention to a common sound.

That said, not all sounds are pleasant. In these cases, we may want to figure out which sounds put us on edge by paying attention to how we feel throughout the day. If our workplace has a lot of background noise, we might see if there's a way to move our desk. In some jobs, we might be able to listen to headphones. We can add white noise: a small fountain, a fish tank, or fan can help a lot in blocking out further away sounds like other people's conversations.

And then there's shopping. I don't like stores that play loud music (and in the winter, I'd rather not hear weeks of mediocre holiday music.) I do most of my shopping at stores that play music more to my taste or at times the store is quiet. It makes my errands much less stressful.

Choosing Sound

While some sounds are outside our control, we can choose many of the sounds we hear each day. We can set our alarm clock sounds, and choose what music we listen to. We can even decide to turn everything off for a while.

I stop and think every few months about what sounds I'm bringing into my home. Some sounds help us see the world in a new way, ask questions, or get a different perspective. Others put people down for fun or encourage us to be passive and not think about the deeper issues. Which one do you want to bring into your life and home? You don't need to stop watching everything—just be aware of what you're watching or listening to and what it's reinforcing.

The same is true of the news. We want to know what's going on, but listening to the news can also be stressful. I limit how much I listen, and instead spend more time with analysis or shows focused on a particular topic. If there's a major news event, I turn on the news for fifteen minutes every few hours. I stay up to date, but I'm not overwhelmed. I use online sources to fill in any gaps.

We can also choose our music. One option with many magical and ritual applications is to create playlists (before MP3s, I made lots of mix tapes and CDs). Some are designed for a long-term focus. When I was working on a series of elemental attunements that lasted months at a time, I created a playlist for each element, full of songs that made me think of that element or that held some related idea. Each list now has at least three hours of music. While I was working on those attunements, I listened to very little outside of that element's list. It kept my attention tightly focused.

My air list includes songs about ravens, music, communication, creativity, and making choices. My fire list has songs about people and their passions, about courage, bravery, love, and willpower. The water list has songs about seals and shipwrecks and everything from rain to streams to oceans. But it also includes songs about intuition, dreams, and memories. And the earth list includes not only songs about animals and rocks, but about seasonal cycles and life cycles. I also have a list for spirit.

Those aren't the only lists I keep, though. I have playlists for each sabbat. When I'm cleaning, I listen to bouncy and energetic songs that also reflect the feeling I want in my home. I make playlists for specific ritual needs, ongoing spells, or when I'm preparing for ritual. I have lists for moving meditation work and to help keep me focused when I'm writing. And I have one playlist I keep for lousy moods: it has songs that reliably make me smile, laugh, or simply relax.

It takes me about twenty minutes to create the base of a list: I scroll through my music and start dropping items in. I then add new things as they occur to me. I listen to most of my lists via the random function (so that order isn't a consideration), but on ritual playlists, I sometimes structure them to build and then release the focus I have in mind. Once they're created, they don't take much management. Pick the one you want that day, and start listening. You may find your playlists turn into a sort of divination tool: the songs that play may turn out to have special meaning for a current concern.

Using sound this way works best when the music speaks deeply to you. While a lot of what I listen to is from folk or pagan music sources, my genres range from medieval music to heavy metal to musicals. Use what makes you respond and what you enjoy.

You'll find some songs bring up strong emotions or memories, or stop you dead in your tracks with their beauty. Use these cautiously: a song like this can jar you out of the mood you want if you use them in the wrong place. I've also found that sometimes listening to a particular song too often can reduce its impact. Be conscious of the effect of each song you choose, and make changes if you need to.

Finally, choose to make space for quiet. Silence first thing in the morning or just before going to bed gives you a chance to tune into your own mind and feelings without distractions. That's a powerful tool, even if it's a little scary sometimes.

Think about what sounds you want to have break that quiet. Use your alarm clock to set the mood for your day by playing music that reminds you of your goals, values, or simply of the beauty of the world. If you're a heavy sleeper, consider having music start about 15 minutes before you want to wake up, and set a loud, annoying alarm for your wake-up time. Your body will gradually wake up with the music, and the loud alarm will jar you less.

Make Your Own Music

Making music is intimate. Our very breath rises and falls with the song we're creating, and we can't help but focus deeply on the music. Listening is useful, but making our own music is magic. You don't have to be perfect. You don't need a trained voice or a great sense of rhythm or pitch. For personal work, all that matters is that you can get into the song and work with it. The rest will come with practice.

Get familiar with your instrument first, and then begin exploring melodies and rhythms as your intuition guides you.

Chants are one of the best ways to get started since all you need is you and your voice. Chants are short, generally two- to four-line songs with simple melodies intended for use in ritual or personal devotion. You may already know a few. If you don't, a search in your favorite online search engine for "pagan chant" will turn up many. Your favorite esoteric store probably sells some chant CDs as well.

Think about your current personal goals and pick a chant that fits your needs. If you want balance in your life, consider a chant relating to the elements. Consider chants that honor a particular deity or focus on a season. You may feel drawn to a particular chant for a reason you don't quite understand. And of course, you can write your own chants for your specific needs.

Remember that learning a chant and using it in your own practice are two different things. You can't truly lose yourself in the chant's song until you stop stumbling over the tune or the words. Try reciting the words by themselves a few times, then sing the tune on "la" to get the notes. When you're comfortable, combine them. If you have a recording, put the song on repeat and sing along. Gradually turn down the volume of the recording until it's just you singing.

You might sing in the morning as part of a devotional practice in front of your altar. You could pick a chant to help you focus or shield yourself and repeat it (under your breath or inside your head) when you need that help. You might use a chant as part of a cleansing bath or shower or as a prayer to your gods before you fall asleep. You might hum it while you exercise or sing while you clean your house or cook.

You can also work with instruments: drums, harps, and flutes are all particularly associated with magic and trance, but any instrument will work. Get familiar with your instrument first, and then begin exploring melodies and rhythms as your intuition guides you. You may want to start with an existing chant or song as your base, and explore from there. If you're interested in drumming, many festivals and larger areas have drum circles and people who would be glad to get you started.

Many people have also looked at how different rhythms, musical scales, or types of melodies affect us. While this can be a dense and complicated subject, books about music and the brain, as well

as books on music theory will have more information that will give you many new kinds of music to explore.

Whichever ways you choose to bring music into your path, play with them. Try out new songs, new expressions, new uses. Pay attention to how each affects you and your focus. Over time, you'll develop a rich understanding of sound and have many ways to focus your intention and goals through music. Most of all, enjoy yourself!

Jenett Silver *is a witch in the Twin Cities and a priestess of a coven with a strong focus on music and the arts in ritual. A librarian by profession, she can generally be found with her nose in a book or at the computer. Her blog (with much more about her and her interests) can be found at http://gleewood.org/threshold/*

Illustrations: Rik Olson

Color Magick

Raven Digitalis

The world is a living tapestry of vibrant color. Magickal and spiritual traditions across the world realize that every color of the rainbow evokes specific energies, including feelings, memories, and associative symbolism. Though most readers of this almanac are familiar with neopagan associations of colors, reading this article may serve both as a good refresher and a platform to expand personal associations with various color energies utilized in daily life and personal spellcraft.

Colors act as part of a symbolic code encompassing acute energetic attributes.

Colors are used in magick to attune to specific vibrations. They also have chakra associations according to Hinduism and are aligned to parts of the human body. Hermeticism and other mystical paths also strongly utilize color symbolism and association. For example, modern esoteric  Qabalah associates precise colors with precise levels of existence, as displayed in the paths and sephiroth on the Tree of Life.

Colors can be used for any magickal purpose. While occult associations of colors are valuable, colors also resonate with individually constructed meanings. We unconsciously judge certain colors and, throughout our life, gain a variety of reactions to them. This is because we understand the symbolism of the color itself on a psychological level. If you associate a particular color with a specific feeling and believe it could be beneficial in spellwork, utilize those personal associations rather than strictly sticking to the book and relying on the associations of other individuals or traditions.

Perhaps, while you were growing up, your friend or relative had a green painted house, and he or she has now requested your help in sending healing energies. In that case, because you associate green with his or her energy pattern, burning a green candle or wearing green clothes in a ritual may be the most appropriate method of achieving this insofar as using color for magickal focus. Or, perhaps you've never been a fan of the color brown and you associate it with icky nastiness. If that is the case, it may be more beneficial for you to use a brown candle in a banishing ritual rather than a black one. At the same time, the colors brown and black represent the colors of the earth (alongside green), so it could also be appropriate to use a candle of one of these colors if the spell is focused on giving unwanted energies back to Mother Earth to transform. The former example demonstrates personal symbolism, while the latter demonstrates common metaphysical associations.

Colors take many different forms in magickal use and are not restricted to a cast circle. The essences of colors can be honed by using colored candles, robes, inks, herbs, stones, feathers, shells, and other materials of focus. If one particular color is emphasized in magick, the emphasized color is allowed to shine as its own distinct, and even exalted, frequency.

For example, wearing mostly dark blue through the day could be intended with the purpose of gaining peace and wisdom. The more you glance at or surround yourself with a color throughout the day, the more its energy will be added to your own energy field because of the mind's reaction to the eyes visually meeting the color. Or the color blue could, in meditation, be envisioned surrounding the throat chakra to heal a sore throat. One can also burn and focus on a blue candle during a ritual to strengthen the healing energy along with the visualization, allowing the fullness of the color to emerge. The possibilities are endless.

Try immersing yourself in a variety of colors, one day at a time. This will merge your own energy pattern with that of the color and helps you get to know the color and its energy—and more importantly, its impact on your psyche and energy body—which will allow for more magickal creativity. It is ideal to align these "color immersions" astrologically, as per the color associated with any given day of the week. They are as follows:

Sunday—Sun: Yellow

Monday—Moon: Violet (or white)

Red

Red is the most primal color, being the color of blood and the base chakra. Red is associated with deep and passionate love. It is the color in ritual that helps the user connect to the innermost part of the self and work with issues of the past, especially emotional wounds based in harmful sexual or aggressive experiences. Red represents the element fire, which stands for passion, vigor, drive, and motivation. It is the driving force for any project or endeavor and can aid in magick dealing with health and physical performance. (This should be performed alongside necessary work on the physical plane, of course.) Additionally, red is a color of life and vitality and can be used to promote wellness. In fact, one death ritual in Madagascar requires mourners to dress in red to encourage the well-being of the deceased.

Pink

Pink, being a lighter hue of red, carries subtler associations than its intense red cousin. Whereas red can represent passionate love, anger, and aggression, pink can be seen as a lesser emanation of these forces. Pink is often associated with vibrations of friendship and can be used in magick to draw friends and comrades. In this sense, the energy of friendship is a lesser (but not less valuable) emanation of red's strong energy. On an associative level, associations of red with anger can be transferred onto pink: perhaps pink, being a lighter shade, can be used to quell and temper the energy of aggression in a magickal working of peace and resolution.

Orange

Orange is the color of strength and endurance. Because of its associations with courage, it can be used in magick to ensure buoyancy and success. Orange represents passionate motivation and honest strength; it is attuned to personal willpower and self-confidence. It can be used to strengthen any magick dealing with employment or the legal system and is a color associated with justice and balance. Qabalists may also associate this color with communication, trade, and anything else Mercurial. Orange is also used for alleviating depression and has associations with the reproductive system.

Yellow

Yellow is the color of the Sun and can be used for guidance and illumination. Its essence is upbeat and generally positive. Yellow represents self-worth and confidence and can help someone come to know himself or herself on a spiritual quest. It is representative of the element air and has associations of mental alertness, intellect, and memory. It's ideal to burn a yellow candle when studying for an exam or researching a topic such as the occult. Yellow also has associations with emotional health.

Green

Green is the color of the earth. It can be utilized in any earthworking and is ideal in natural magick. It is grounding and stabilizing; empowering and sustaining. Green is the color of growth and flourishing and is used in fertility magick, especially during the sabbats. If used in conjunction with the waxing Moon, the essence of spiritual growth lends itself to personal magick. It is the ideal time to work magick concerning new beginnings and interests. Westerners tend to associate green with fiscal factors like money, prosperity, and mundane success. It's a perfect color to use in working toward these ends because, certainly, we significantly rely on the material plane as the plateau for jumping to higher ground.

Blue

Blue is a color of peace and expansion. Its calming tones can aid in settling disputes. It invites equanimity and tranquility to any situation and is an aid in the healing process. Because of its tranquil nature, blue is a color of meditation and finding harmony in chaos, and it ensures safety in travel. It can be used to conduct creative and mindful energies in study, writing, communication, and art. Blue is associated with divine love and mercy. It is the rarest color in the plant and animal worlds, yet it is the color of the illuminated ocean and sky. Therefore, blue can be used for universal magick and expanding your own energy outward. It can be used to discover something "rare" from lost objects to secrets of the planes. It is also a good color to work with, alongside black, when feeling blue, depressed, or despondent. It is said to be the color of the dream world and can be used in any sleep or astral working. Many witches also believe that blue is the best color to use for energetic protection.

Indigo

A number of people report strong, swirling visions of the color indigo when performing deep meditation—myself included! This makes sense, as indigo is the color of the third eye, or Ajna chakra. Because of this connection, indigo is associated with the psychic arts. The color indigo appears as a vibrant combination of blue and violet. Using this color in magick aids the development of psychic awareness, intuition, and divinatory ability. Indigo is the color of total spiritual attunement. Many people believe the color to be the strongest spiritual color, next only to black and white. Indigo may also be associated with mental states and moods, again because of the chakra connection. It can be used in spirit communication, protective magick, and transcendental meditation with the aim of uncovering ancient truths.

Violet

Because it is a combination of red (a fast color) and blue (a slow color), violet represents total balance, perhaps even of mastery of the physical realm. Because it is a color between two extremes, it's perfect to use when seeing "through the veil" in divinatory work, trance, and meditation. Qabalistic lunar associations also lend credence in this definition. Violet/purple may also be used to bring a situation back to its original peaceful state and is good to work with when trying to bring an immediate situation back into balance. Like indigo, violet is used in meditation and helps in transcendental spiritual work. It is the highest color of the rainbow that the human eye can perceive at this time and represents high states of consciousness. Violet may be used to psychically navigate the body to find any imbalances and help to heal ailments. It helps restore the body to its natural state as a healing, sensory system, and it aids the magician in working toward full-body wellness.

White

According to New Age circles, white is a color of ascension and of the heavenly realms. It is a vast and versatile color, taking on the meaning of peace, happiness, and healing in some cultures; and death, mourning, and astral matter according to other cultures. White can be used to deflect harm and is, therefore, protective. Its "white light" healing attributes are aplenty in metaphysical energy work. As the energy of the color can benefit any area of the body and any layer of the soul, it is the most "multipurpose" color of them all. White is absolute light and can be used for guidance and the initiative of positive change. It illuminates clarity in any given circumstance. White is adaptable and may be substituted for any other color, should its energy not be immediately available for spellcasting, meditation, prayer, or what-have-you. It is the color of the Moon (from Earth's vantage point) and represents lunar connection for witches and others who observe the lunar tides. It represents serenity and clarity and is a color of spiritual cleansing. White is also associated with happiness and general well-being.

Black

The color black represents numerous things just as much as its equal-opposite color white. Though the darkness is frequently associated with fear, the color black has numerous sacred associations that must not be forgotten. Black is a color of creation—every creation myth across countless cultures begins with blackness. It is from the darkness that the light of consciousness is born, and this energy can be utilized by any magician, which is one reason why magick performed at nighttime is so powerful. Black is heavily associated with spiritual protection—you know, the whole "cloak of invisibility." The color black can be utilized in any protective (or baneful) magick. It is also associated with mourning, death, and dying in modern culture, so black can be utilized in ancestral communication, deathworkings, and necromantic rites of any type. Black represents the dark and fertile soil and can, as was mentioned in terms of creation mythology, be used for planting energetic seeds and growing energies of benefit.

Gray

The color gray is a combination of black and white, therefore encompassing both colors' energies. Gray is the color of ashes and neutrality and can be used to bring a situation or area back to a state of balance. Gray is the color of the Qabalistic Middle Pillar of Equilibrium, which is also called the Pillar of Balance, of Consciousness and of Benignity. Gray represents all of these things, and a magician working with Qabalistic magick can use gray to align with the total balance the Middle Pillar represents. Gray is associated with meditation and vision-seeking. Its essence falls into no extreme; it's not entirely black or white, warm or cold, fast or slow. It is the ideal color to magickally utilize when seeking a state of restorative balance. Gray represents everything and nothing, all at once. It is the primary color of wizardry, representing equilibrium—a mastery of the planes.

Brown

The color brown, in addition to green, is highly representative of the element earth. Like black, brown can also be used to represent the soil, and can, thus, be honed in ritual to plant energetic seeds of spiritual growth. Brown, green, and black are the primary colors of earth, so any magick working directly with this element (consider the metaphysical associations of earth) can benefit from the use of these colors within the rite. Additionally, the color brown is specifically associated with animal magick. When working any type of animal magick (the most common being healing for a pet), it is of benefit to burn a brown candle, wear a brown robe, or utilize the color in another manner when weaving energy to do with the animal kingdom.

Raven Digitalis (*Missoula*, MT) *is the author of* Shadow Magick Compendium: Exploring Darker Aspects of Magickal Spirituality *and* Goth Craft: The Magickal Side of Dark Culture, *both at Llewellyn. He is a neopagan priest and cofounder of the Disciplined Eclectic, a shadow magick tradition; and the training coven Opus Aima Obscuræ. Raven holds a degree in anthropology from the University of Montana. He is a radio and club DJ of Gothic, EBM, and industrial music; he is also an animal rights activist, and black-and-white photographic artist. He has appeared on the cover of* newWitch *magazine, is a regular contributor to* The Ninth Gate *magazine, and has been featured on MTV News and the 'X' Zone Radio program. Raven's Web sites include: www.ravendigitalis.com and www.myspace.com/oakraven*

Illustrations: Tim Foley

Twenty-first Century Glamours

Phaedra Bonewits

Once upon a time, and by complete chance, two boys met face to face for the first time. With a shock, each one realized that it was as if he were not looking at another boy, but into a mirror. Each boy was the other's twin—in all respects, save one. One boy was a prince, the other a pauper. Each had experiences the other could never know. Boys being boys, whether rich or poor, they conceived a daring plan: to change clothes and live for a day like the other.

Once upon a time, two girls from two different worlds met, only to discover they are long-separated twins.

They hatched a plan to meet the mother (for one) and the father (for the other) that they never knew, by switching clothes and switching places.

The first story, as I'm sure you recognized, comes from Mark Twain's *The Prince and the Pauper*; the second is the plot of the Disney movie *The Parent Trap*. Each story hinges on a transformation effected by a change of clothes. As a kid, I wondered why no one noticed anything different about the children. I mean, they spoke and acted different from the other. It takes a while for even the parents of the girls to see past their surface resemblances. But the pauper didn't know how to act like a prince, and people persisted in treating him based on the way he was dressed. The same with the prince; no matter how loudly he declared himself to be royal, he was treated like the commoner his clothes declared him to be.

Stranger still, changing their clothing changed the boys themselves. The scruffy pauper adapted to the grandeur that people expected from him, while the prince became more humble and less demanding as he learned of the harsh life outside the royal court. These are mere stories, of course, but stories that would not be half so interesting if we did not believe such transformations could be accomplished.

Playwrights, novelists, and filmmakers have always understood the importance of the clothes their characters wear. Masks and costume tell the audience immediately not just what the character is—this is Lion King and that's a gazelle—but what to think about the character. He's dressed like a biker so don't mess with him. She's wearing a pink, frilly dress, so she's a girly-girl. He's in a three-piece suit, so he must be in charge.

It works so well because we are hard-wired to believe our eyes. "Seeing is believing," we say or "What you see is what you get." Our brains cheerfully and efficiently assign data to categories we already

have in place. We associate certain roles and attributes to people based on the way they look, the way they dress, or the way they move.

Most of the time, it works pretty well. So well, in fact, that we seldom go any further than what we see. Thus, much of our entertainment drama revolves around characters behaving in unexpected ways given what we have been made to believe about them from looking at their clothing. The biker is a softie inside. The girl in the frilly dress has a black belt in karate. The guy in the three-piece suit works in the mailroom and aspires to be in charge. But what about those real-life dramas? And how is this important to the modern magical practitioner? Well, the prince, the pauper, the sisters, and the actors have used clothes to cast a glamour, a spell, a bewitchment, or enchantment that causes people to see someone or something differently over those around them.

We've seen some of this in movies that purport to be about magic, such as when the girls in *The Craft* wave their hands around and change their hair and eye color. The wizards and witches in Harry Potter books and movies make it a bit more work by taking months to brew a potion, add a bit of hair from someone, and (swish! flick!) take on the appearance of the other person. But even our Hogwarts students cannot complete their transformation without donning the appropriate clothing. Even if their faces and bodies look like Slytherin boys, they won't get access to the Slytherin tower dressed in Gryffindor robes.

For we who do not have access to special "powers" or boomslang skin, it is surprisingly easy to mimic our fictional friends. Anyone who has access to hair dye and colored contact lenses can do what *The Craft* girls did (albeit not quite so quickly). Certainly, any young lady who has dressed for the prom has practiced this magic. "Bewitching," we call her. She looks "enchanting." Her date is "spellbound."

In fact, changing clothes changes our appearance so radically that it is the simplest magical tool we have. So much so, in fact, that con men and other deceivers have taken advantage of our willingness to believe what we see (and see what we expect to see) from time immemorial. But clothing glamour has positive applications, too. For example, we all know we should dress up for a job interview—but not too much. We show up in clothes appropriate for the job we wish to get, and those who do not are less likely to get the job.

This is glamour magic on two levels. First, the clothing itself casts a glamour on the ones who see it: Oh, look! That person is appropriate for this job. In the same way, we usually dress appropriately for a wedding, or school, or out clubbing, even if, like the pauper in the prince's finery, we feel silly or out of place. ("I will never wear an outfit like this again in my life!") As long as we look the part, we are treated as the bride, the student, the nightlife seeker, or the probable right person for the job.

Secondly, the change of clothing begins to change us, too. We look in the mirror and say, Yep, I look like an account executive. It gives us a little more confidence, no matter how much we may be quaking inside. The bride looks in the mirror and sees herself as the "Bride." Wow. Her posture may change or her language and manners may become a tad more formal. She feels special, a little larger than life, for this one day.

Being in or out of a uniform has a similar effect. Military people wear uniforms and so do mail carriers, maintenance workers, nurses, and countless others. A three-piece suit is a kind of uniform, too; one that's darn hard to kick back and relax in while wearing. Uniforms nudge us toward the behavior that is expected from a person in that outfit. When we get home, we change into the clothes that (magically) say to us and those around us: "I'm off duty now, it's time to be something else."

Clothing can also function in the same way as amulets and talismans. An amulet (an object) or a talisman (something written) is designed to attract or repel certain energies. Clothing, jewelry, makeup, and certainly tattoos can all function as amulets or talismans.

Years ago, I had a favorite hairdresser who wore her hair in a huge, spiky mohawk, used red eyeshadow, and dusted her face with black blusher. She was a really sweet gal (and cut my hair great), but I knew if I ran into her in a dark alley, I'd have been sure she was ready to pull out a razor to cut something besides my hair. The same goes for a black outfit with lots of chains and studs. It functions as an amulet of protection, since most people will not want to have a confrontation with the person who dresses like that. The brain reads the eye's data and says, "Better safe than sorry!" After all, even if part of our brain suspects that inside he or she may be just a pussycat, by the time we found out for sure it might be too late.

We also wear clothes to attract people to us, not necessarily in the "I'm hot, date me!" sense, but in the "I am a person like you, so come hang out with me" sense. I know when I see people wearing a pentacle or a Druid sigil that I'll strike up a conversation with someone I might never have otherwise. Tattoos are especially potent talismans in this regard. A person might wear a piece of jewelry without understanding the symbolism, but a permanent mark is a clearly magical design that would only be worn if it was meaningful to them.

When designing a spell you can use your clothes and accessories as magical tools. For example, if you are casting a spell to find a job, include your interview clothes in the spellcasting. Try giving them a shot of extra-attention energy so you'll be noticed among a crowd of perhaps equally qualified applicants. Charge them just as you would a more conventional talisman or amulet.

In more formal ritual work, either magical or religious, clothing can also enhance or detract from your results. Our daily experiences tell us that any time we take extra effort with something, it affects the results. We all know that dinner made by tossing something in the microwave is not quite as savory as one that took a good deal of time to prepare from scratch. However nice the microwave results are, they are not the same. A meal set on a table is a combination of the ingredients and the efforts of the cook. Our appreciation of those efforts (whether our own or someone else's) adds to the flavor.

Clearly, anything we do with extra effort, whether it's cooking, schoolwork, practicing the piano, or dressing for a special occasion, leads to more satisfactory results. The effort we take not only improves our skills, as with schoolwork or piano playing, it actually stimulates our brains to appreciate the result more. Thus, when we make the effort to change our appearance for ritual or magical work, we are, just as the bride in her gown, sending a message to our brains that this is a very special occasion that is meant to be taken very seriously.

Of course, one gets married just as legally at the courthouse in casual wear, and one can do magic in ritual in any old clothes. But think about the message we're sending our inner selves. If we wear the same clothes to ritual as we wore to the grocery store earlier in the afternoon, are we saying the ritual is no more important than, or different from, going to the grocery store? Is that what you really believe?

How we dress indicates to both ourselves and to others how much importance we attach to a particular occasion, as well as how much respect we have for others on that occasion. Showing up in blue jeans at a formal wedding certainly makes a statement, but most people will read that statement as something of an insult to the bride and groom. If, on the other hand, you dress in a manner far more elaborate than that of the wedding party, you send the message that you feel you are more important today than they are.

And if we show up in either blue jeans or over-elaborate dress in error, we might feel mortified. Just about everyone has the dream where you find yourself inappropriately dressed or not dressed at all. The anxiety nightmares such as those produce are a good measure of how deeply we feel a need to be in the "correct" clothing.

With group ritual and magical work, we can take advantage of the ability of special clothing to make us either stand out or fit in. If everyone is dressed alike, it creates the mindset that we're all on the same team. That's what team uniforms are all about, after all. Even if clothing is only similar—for example, everyone is in prom clothes or bathing suits or business suits—it still sends the message that we're all part of a group with a common agenda. For this reason, most covens or other magical working groups choose to have everyone wear similar garb, with flowing robes of some sort being the most popular choice. Why robes? Why not matching sweatsuits or business suits or prom dresses? The answer is a little complex.

We have very deep cultural associations between religion and flowing garments. For millennia, our gods and goddesses have been represented in draped and flowing garments. Even the Christian images of Jesus are frozen, artistically, in the drapery of the Roman Empire. Our modern religious experiences include the Pope in robes, the Dalai Lama in robes, choirs in robes, Gandhi in a shoulder drape, nuns in habits, preachers in vestments, and on and on. All these images create associations in our minds, *whether we are consciously aware of them or not*, with loose, flowing clothing and religious authority.

Thus, the donning of a robe is a psychological trigger that helps our brains shift from an everyday, ordinary state of consciousness to a more magical, religious state of mind. Just as the bride looks in the mirror and sees the Bride, when we can don our full magical regalia and look into the mirror, we see not just someone dressed for running errands, we see the witch!

In fact, many groups have the custom of treating each other with special courtesy and respect while they are dressed in their robes as a way of reinforcing the magical state of mind. When the group's mood begins to swing back to more ordinary consciousness, people know

it's time to get out of the robes and back into everyday clothing. In this way, extra oomph is added to the psychological trigger so that merely changing out of their mundane clothing and into ritual gear assists their minds and psyches to make the shift into ritual space, too.

For larger workings, you can also exploit the ability of clothing to make certain people stand out from the crowd. The high priest and high priestess of the ritual may have special headgear or different accessories to set them apart and make them more visible. Other facilitators may wear attention-getting clothing to indicate, at a glance, that they are song leaders, or Officers of the Quarters, or whatever else their role may be.

Of course, it may not always be practical or desirable to dress in full ritual garb. Simple items, such as special scarves, shawls, or shirts can also set the mood, especially if they have been set aside for ritual use only and not used for any other purpose.

A tabard is especially handy for this purpose. It's a simple, one-piece garment that probably looks most like a long, skinny, rectangular poncho. It has an opening for your head, but no sleeves or side seams. Slip it over your head and whatever you're wearing becomes transformed into ritual garb. Some groups use special tabards to indicate the roles people will play in a ritual. A high priestess tabard, for example, will make her role immediately obvious to other participants and will help her get into her role just by putting it on.

What about the witches who don't wear clothes at all? Going skyclad is an option for both groups and individuals. There are many explanations for why some Wiccans work skyclad, some more convincing than others. But it is a powerful example of clothing magic. After all, we spend most of our time clothed. Most people even wear some kind of clothing when they sleep. We have powerful cultural taboos against being seen in clothing designated as underwear (even if bathing suits can be even skimpier), much less entirely naked. The act of removing all your clothes in front of others becomes an immense act of trust; and, since it is a complete break from ordinary behavior, the lack of clothing becomes magically potent.

Of course, even those who work skyclad are never completely naked—where would we Wiccans be without our jewelry? It becomes our amulets, talismans, clothing, and . . . oh, look, shiny stuff!

Phaedra Bonewits *has been making magic and leading ritual for more that two decades. She occasionally shares the spotlight with her husband, Isaac, with whom she co-authored her book* Real Energy. *Phaedra has a background in fine art, and a special interest in Tarot and transformational magic.*

Illustrations: Kathleen Edwards

Magical Transformations

EVERYTHING OLD IS NEW AGAIN

Magick and Science: The Veil is Thinning!

Susan Pesznecker

Magick and science have long been at odds, at least in the eyes of the non-magickal world. A scientist looks at Mars, sees a rocky red planet that might be colonized in the future, investigates its scientific properties, and decries any claim that mystical energies might be part of its nature. People who use magick view Mars as a fierce, masculine, passionate presence that influences via felt energies and astrological positions—a presence that influences our daily lives in ways we feel scientists have yet to appreciate or understand. Examples like this frame the argument between science and magick.

In some ways, the gap seems unbreachable. The scientific method relies on empirical study, with scientists employing objective means to study and describe natural phenomena and using the results to establish theories and recreate their findings. "Good science" is only valid if it's reproducible. In contrast, subjective experiences, such as revelation, inspiration, and reflection, help people better understand life and magick in terms of their own religion and spirituality. Further, each person's experiences with magick are unique. An old axiom says that science relies on facts and religion on faith—but the situation is much more complex than that. Most magick users view themselves as not just observing what's happening around them, but as willing to see and examine at a deeper level and practice with an open-minded, wonder-based approach to the world around them. In the magickal universe, something doesn't have to occur repetitively in order to be believed. Simply said, scientists tend to believe in evidence, while magick users tend to believe their eyes.

One of the simplest demonstrations of this dichotomy can be seen with energy. To scientists, energy is a physical system that allows living beings to "do work." Whether kinetic, thermal, or in one of many other forms, energy follows a simple law of conservation, which says that while it can change form, the total energy remains unchanged. Scientists are eminently concerned with managing energy and making it do what they want it to do. In contrast, magick users work cooperatively with energy, in a synergistic partnership. We cast it out into the universe via spellwork and ritual and pull it down around us when we meditate or set a shield. We manipulate energy every time we call down the moon or balance a chakra, and we understand the checks and balances involved in the laws of conservation, whether pulling strength from the universe or returning the excess back to Mother Gaia. To magick users, the relationships between science, energy, and magick are obvious: the Force is, indeed, all around

us. Yet, most scientists struggle with the idea that humans might manipulate and use energy on an immediate, personal level.

The world's history books document centuries of perceived disparity between science and magick, and the earliest humans may have understood magick better than any modern human ever has. To the Neoliths, magick and the supernatural were part of the fabric of everyday life, with gods to be appeased and goddesses appealed to. The Egyptians worshipped their own Pantheon, while the Romans originally embraced a rich polytheistic tradition before adopting Christianity as the official state belief. The Chinese have a long, rich history of manipulating the energy they know as Qi ("chee"), practices that continue in their modern culture today. Medieval Europeans, caught up in the great struggle between the old pagan religions and the advent of Christianity, viewed magick and natural forces as being somewhere between necessary, frightening, and heretical. Although the Enlightenment opened up our collective consciousness and pushed us to ask questions and question assumptions, the modern trend is one of skepticism with regard to magick and the supernatural. If we consider human history to be one long continuum, it appears that twenty-first-century Western civilization has lost its childlike sense of wonder.

Despite people's cynicism, modern times are filled with wonder. Science today tells us that time travel may be possible, alternate dimensions may be real, and the universe around us may be built of mysterious dark matter that we believe is there but we can't really see. Invisibility may be real, levitation possible, and gravity flexible. Yet science continues to decry magick as an imaginary product of the New Age, an interesting irony given that science continues to push into the foggy regions of quantum mechanics, where normal physics quit working and progress is mostly theoretical or based on faith. We magick users just nod, knowing we're ahead of our time. But while we wait for the scientific world to catch up, we ponder the thinning boundaries between science and magick and consider the possibilities. Given the choice to see a physical law rewritten, which would we choose? For most of us, the answer is simple: gravity. Who hasn't dreamed of taking flight, of soaring through the sky like a bird, light and carefree? That gravity business, though … it's a tough nut to crack.

Levitation and Gravity

You've all heard the story about Newton's apple … Isaac Newton is wandering about one afternoon and decides to relax under an apple tree. He's sitting there, maybe dozing, when suddenly an apple drops down and thunks him on the head. As the tale goes, this gets Newton to thinking about why everything falls down toward the Earth, instead of falling up, or even sideways. So begins his exploration into the laws of gravity.

What is gravity? Simply said, it's the tendency of two objects with mass to attract one another—in Newton's case, the attraction was between an apple and his head. Mass refers to the actual atomic volume of a piece of matter (i.e., the number of electrons, protons, molecules, and so forth, that comprise an object). Imagine that you had an empty room and put ten people into it. Now imagine the same room filled with fifty people. If the room is analogous to a piece of matter and the people to individual atoms, the room with fifty people has a higher density and a greater mass.

As for weight, it refers to the effect of gravity on a mass-containing object. If a person weighs 120 pounds on Earth, under 1g (the force created by Earth's gravitational field), she'll weigh 20 pounds on the Moon, where gravity is only $\frac{1}{6}$ g. But her mass will be exactly the same on Earth and the Moon, because her atomic volume—and relative density—haven't changed.

Newton wasn't the first scientist to think about gravity: ancient philosophers pondered the problem as well. Humans originally believed that the heavens revolved around the Earth, a theory known as "geocentric," or Earth-centered. In the early 1600s, Copernicus advanced his theories of heliocentricism and his proof that the Sun was at the center of the solar system. Labeled an apostate, Copernicus served prison time for these findings, which were seen as dangerously heretical. Interestingly, the word "heretic" comes to us from the Greek *hairetikos*, literally "able to choose." Copernicus chose to set aside faith-based geocentricism and introduced a science-based view of the universe, choosing to subvert the Church's control in favor of truth and, thereby, laying the groundwork for centuries that followed.

Galileo Galilei made another step toward understanding gravity in the late 1600s, when he dropped balls of different weights from the top of the Tower of Pisa and made deductions about the relationship between mass and acceleration. The results convinced him that gravity affected all objects equally, a major departure from earlier theories in which gravity was believed to be influenced by an object's mass and weight.

Copernicus and Galileo were among those setting the stage for Newton's greatest work: his law of universal gravitation. This law found that all mass-containing objects were affected by gravity in a predictable and constant fashion. Along with this, Newton developed three laws of motion, which helped explain gravity and its effects.

Newton's first law of motion is the law of inertia, which says that objects at rest tend to stay at rest, while those in motion tend to keep moving. Imagine you're riding in a car that brakes suddenly. The car slows to a rapid stop, but your body keeps moving, surging against the seat belt. You're in motion, and Newton's law is trying to keep you moving; the only reason you stop is because

the seat belt holds you to the stopping car. How does this law work for magick users? Imagine the feeling as you begin to raise a cone of power during ritual. It takes some work to get the power going, but once it begins, it's hard to hold back, and once it's raised, it's equally hard to disperse.

Newton's second law describes the relationship between mass and motion, via position, direction, velocity, speed, and acceleration. Position refers to an object's fixed location in space, while direction implies movement from one position toward another. Velocity is the rate of change of position, while speed is a measurement defining how quickly something moves from one position to another. Finally, acceleration is the rate of change of velocity.

Calculating velocity requires both speed and direction, while acceleration can be affected by either speed *or* direction. Acceleration can also be "negative." We tend to think that accelerating means going faster. But acceleration is the rate of *change* of velocity, in either speed or direction. A car that slows down or turns is accelerating just as a car that speeds up.

To understand Newton's second law, we need one more term: momentum. Momentum refers to the quantity of motion of a moving body, measured as a product of its mass and velocity. Okay: imagine you wad up a single sheet of paper and throw it. You can accelerate the paper wad at a decent speed, but it has a very low mass, therefore, its momentum is low. It won't go far and will quickly decelerate and fall to the ground. Now imagine you pick up a book and throw it, using the same approximate force used to throw the paper wad. The acceleration is more difficult and is less than the paper wad, because the book has a higher mass. But because of that mass, the book's momentum is greater than that of the paper wad; thus, the book may go further than the wad, and when it hits the ground, it skids before stopping.

Last but not least is Newton's third law, which proves that every action generates an equal and opposite reaction. Shoot a gun and you feel the recoil. Magick users work with the action-reaction law any time we send energy out into the universe, because we know that the energy or spell must be sent with good intention, for whatever we send out bounces back into our laps—and the greater the spell's momentum, the more likely we'll feel its impact.

We also understand the limits of gravity. Stories of witches zooming about on broomsticks took flight during the medieval witch hysteria but met a nicer turn in recent years, when Harry Potter and friends climbed onto their Nimbus 2000s and took to the skies. Who among us wouldn't love to ride a broom or step into a wormhole or zip across the universe, tesseract-style? We content ourselves with dream work, guided meditation, and astral journeying, but how wonderful it would be to swoop through the clouds or explore the stars.

Light Speed and Time Travel

Newton's laws revolutionized science, and they still hold up today. In the twentieth century, Einstein followed with his general theory of relativity by relating gravitational effects to the curved dimension of "spacetime" rather than to rigid linear physics, flirting with the perceived barriers of light speed and vast distance.

Einstein would be happy to hear that traveling at warp speed may one day become reality. In August 2008, scientists at Baylor University in Texas advanced a new theory that could allow space vehicles to exceed light speed, while still cooperating with Newton's and Einstein's laws. Their theory suggests that manipulating the extra-spatial dimensions of string theory around a spaceship could create a "bubble" that could effectively allow the ship to travel "outside" of gravity, moving faster than the speed of light. (String theory is a type of theoretical physics proposing that the universe is created of one-dimensional strings. Strings behave and intersect in unique ways that support quantum physics and novel approaches to gravitation.) Guided by the strings, space-time would effectively expand behind the spaceship and shrink in front of it, pushing the bubble along. Since known space would continue to move around the ship, the theory wouldn't violate Einstein's laws of space-time curvature but would move between them.

The Baylor theory would require enormous amounts of energy for initiation and acceleration, but once in motion, minimal energy would be needed to sustain the momentum. If spaceships could move faster than light-speed, enormous distances could be crossed in short time periods, making intergalactic travel possible. Even more tantalizing is the idea that human dimensional or galactic travel—as in the ability to propel one's self across the universe—might follow on the heels of "bubble travel."

Invisibility

Next to being able to fly through the sky, most of us would love to possess a good invisibility charm. To be invisible is to be unseeable, and to move and "do" at will. Today's magick users learn to work with energy shields, not only to repel vagrant energy but also to cloak themselves against wandering eyes. The person who casts an invisibility shield charm appears to soften and fade into the background, to become less noticeable. The magick is imperfect but surprisingly effective—even in its simplest form.

Today's scientists have moved closer to creating a real invisibility cloak. In August 2008, scientists at the University of California,

Berkeley, announced they had used "metamaterials" to successfully cloak (and hide!) a three-dimensional object. Metamaterials—a mixture of Teflon, ceramic, and silicon composites—work by bending light and redirecting it around and away from a solid object. We see solid objects because the objects "scatter" the light that strikes them, reflecting the scattered light back to the viewer's eye. If the light is redirected, it can't scatter or create shadows, and the object becomes unseeable. The metamaterials can also scatter radar signals, suggesting the new technology has obvious military implications. But what fun to think we might one day don invisibility cloaks, just like Harry's.

Moving Photos

And speaking of Harry, in the first Harry Potter film we watched, transfixed, as Hagrid presented the boy with a special photo album, in which photos of Harry's long-dead parents hugged and twirled and winked at him. Even a handful of years ago, this seemed marvelous. But digital picture frames have since hit the market, and now we have the ability to watch stills or digital video of loved ones moving across our very own photo-screens. Electronic papers are under development and will allow display of digital stills and video on paper-thin sheets. Digital scrapbooking won't be far behind: imagine the wonders this could add to your Book of Shadows.

Quantum Physics

Time travel, antigravity, and electronic paper aside, the realm of quantum physics is the place where science and magick seem most likely to touch. Quantum physics is the study of dimensional systems whose mechanisms and boundaries exist at or outside of the atomic scale. This means quantum physics operates in regions we know little or nothing about and in ways that often break existing physical laws.

The field of quantum study surpasses both Newton's and Einstein's laws in trying to explain how gravity and physics behave in unknown environments, a discipline that explores the realms of superlight speed and time travel. Let's look at some examples.

Quantum physics says that we live in an observer-dependent universe, with our observation literally creating the reality that we observe. If we can see something, it's real—at least for that moment. In quantum theory, an object's position is continuous rather than fixed and is "smeared out" in relationship to time, allowing objects to be in more than more place at once—at least theoretically. Quantum mechanics also suggests that since we cannot pinpoint an object's exact position at any point in time, we have no way of knowing where it is when we can't see it. Fix your gaze on a lamp across the room. Now, turn your back. According to quantum science, you can't prove that the lamp is still there, for if there's no observer, there's no reality. Magick users have always understood this.

Or consider the quantum jump, which says that objects can disappear from one place and reappear in another without actually crossing the intervening distance. This type of movement describes the physics of electron movement, with electrons moving between orbital shells in an atom. It sounds a lot like L'Engle's tesseract, or Captain Kirk's molecular transporter, doesn't it?

The features of quantum theory cast traditional physics into doubt. The objective universe is still there, but in a quantum setting, its factual objective nature comes increasingly under question because of the observer-dependency of reality. From observer-based reality, it's a quick step to Jung's ideas of synchronicity, literally "meaningful coincidence," where seemingly coincidental occurrences take on observer meaning. Ultimately, magick becomes a more likely and reasonable option in the quantum environment than it ever was in the Newtonian-Einsteinian universe.

The theorist Claude Levi-Strauss once suggested that magick and science were actually two parallel modes of acquiring knowledge and that they were much more similar than different. As quantum study continues to push the edges of what we *think* we know, the distance between magick and science narrows, and our views of what's magick and what's science continue to evolve. For magick users, the coming years will be exciting ones.

Susan "Moonwriter" Pesznecker *has practiced Earth-based spirituality for more than two decades. She earned a master's degree in nonfiction writing, after spending twenty-five years as a nurse, and she switched professions to become a college English teacher. Susan has published* Gargoyles *(Career Press, 2007) and* Crafting Magick with Pen and Ink *(Llewellyn, 2009). Susan teaches at the Grey School of Wizardry and is preparing to open the Earthkeepers School of Green Magick. She lives in Oregon.*

Illustrations: Tina Fong

Live Lightly on the Pagan Path

Dallas Jennifer Cobb

It is a rocky economic time, with consumer debt on the rise, mortgage foreclosures, and instability in the international money markets. Not only do we face increased costs for basic necessities like food and fuel, but the newspapers and media are constantly filled with messages of fear, despair, and dread. "The future doesn't look good," people say, an ominous tone to their words.

Do we really have to believe everything we read or can we cultivate a mindset of gratitude? Can we learn the skills needed to recognize and generate prosperity in our lives during these so-called tough times? Can we focus our intention to create goodness around and in our lives regardless of what is out there in the world?

While there are no miracle solutions to massive debts, a positive pagan practice can put you on the path of living lightly—living with a light energy surrounding you, a light debt load, and of course living lightly on the planet. With a little knowledge of the laws of nature and how they relate to a pagan practice, we can charge our actions with positivity and prosperity, cultivating a life abundant with practical ideas that are solution-oriented. In line with the laws of nature, practicing everyday magic, we can transform our very lives, but in order to "live lightly," we need to understand the nature of light.

The Laws of Nature

If you are like me, you learned about the laws of nature in science classes. Take a moment and think back to your physics teachers who taught the basics—those simple statements that summarize what the universe is made of, how it is organized, and how it works. These laws appear to be universal and can be consistently tested, proven, and reproduced. The laws of nature apply to, and are the basis for, all life on this planet.

With a basic understanding of the laws of nature, we can then understand how they relate to our magical practices, and we can learn to use them to guide our daily living, decision-making, and actions. Aligned with the universal laws of nature, we can benefit from their enormous and irrefutable energy, using them to magnify our magical power and its effect.

The Law of Vibration

The law of vibration says that the universe is made up of energy. Anything that exists in our universe, whether seen or unseen, can be broken down into its purest form, which is energy or light. Each

different energy has a distinct pattern of vibration, or frequency. These patterns can include cycles or rhythms. That means that not just physical things, but also thoughts, feelings, desires, and dreams have a vibration and are affected by larger cyclic patterns.

THE LAW OF ATTRACTION

The law of attraction or resonance states that energy is attracted to like energy, resonance, or vibration. So like attracts like, and opposites repel. This law governs the things, events, and people that come into our lives and reminds us that there is always a response to our thoughts, feelings, words, and actions. The energy that we send out attracts like energies. When we focus on exuding positive energy, we succeed in attracting positive energy to us.

THE LAW OF CAUSE AND EFFECT

The law of cause and effect says that each action has an equal and opposite reaction. Anything that is done will produce results in exact proportion to, or greater than, the action that caused it. Energy cannot be destroyed, but it can be transformed. So consider the effect that your actions may cause and what outcome that effect may bring. Your actions are not benign.

THE LAW OF RECIPROCITY

The law of reciprocity holds that two substances in an interaction give and take mutually in kind or degree. So in an interaction with another person, each of you is affected equally, though not identically. When two cars collide, both are affected, and when two people meet, each feels a response to the other person. No interaction happens within a vacuum, so everything is shared between the two parties involved. Give and take, push and pull, win and lose.

The Law of Action

The law of action states that all action brings results. So we can manifest specific results by acting consciously and with a specific focus. When we dive into the water, the water level rises. When we hammer a nail, it sinks into the wood. Knowing this law, we can choose actions that will create our desired effect. Because the law of action also applies to our thoughts, dreams, emotions, and words we can meditate on someone to promote their healing or well-being, we can cast blessings spells to protect our loved ones, and we can speak kind words to uplift people around us.

The Law of Abundance

The law of abundance reminds us that the universe is continually growing and changing. Knowing this, we can magically affirm that what we focus on, grows. And, affirm that the Goddess loves, us and will provide for us. The law of abundance reminds us that there is no lack in this world.

The Law of Growth

The law of growth relates to the law of abundance and states that what will grow is dependent on the kind and quality of seed that is planted. A tomato will never grow from an apple seed. Good feelings will grow from good thoughts and good words. When we are conscious and purposeful with what we 'sow' in our lives, great goodness is ours to harvest.

The Law of Polarity

The law of polarity states that everything has an opposite. Think of a magnet energetically charged; it is positive at one end and negative at the other. When we find ourselves obsessing on something disturbing, we hold a negative charge. To relieve ourselves of this energy, we can change our thoughts purposefully, consciously choosing to focus on a positive outcome. This simple action can produce a change in polarity, relieving us of negativity.

THE LAW OF PERPETUAL TRANSMUTATION OF ENERGY

The law of perpetual transformation of energy tells us that energy is always changing, so the nature of our universe is change. Applying this law empowers us to change anything in our lives: our selves, our situation, and our reality. By understanding the laws of nature and aligning our actions and magical practice with them, we can bring about miraculous change. Dion Fortune once said, "Magic is the art of changing consciousness at will." Observing the laws of nature can create a change in consciousness and can produce a transformation in our energy and the energy surrounding and affecting us in the universe.

The Pagan Practice

The pagan tradition honors the laws of nature. As practicing pagans we observe **the law of oneness**, acknowledging that everything in this world is connected to everything else. Our universe is one big symbiotic being, so whatever we do affects all of the universe, somehow.

Pagan holy days are tuned into the vibration and rhythm of our universe, honoring the major lunar, solar, and seasonal cycles. And pagans practice magic, informed by the laws of nature, how they order the universe, and influence reality and outcomes. What we learned in science classes guides how we make magic.

Think now of some of the standards you have heard used in the pagan community, both in conversation and in ritual practice. Many of the often-used statements come directly from, and are perhaps based on, the laws of nature. They are recognizable however paraphrased.

We say "what goes around, comes around" and "what you send out into the universe will come back to you three fold." In my circle, when we are in sacred space, we say that we "work magic between the worlds, and this magic affects all worlds." Pagans also hold that ideas, which are mental energy, can manifest in a physical form, saying "be careful what you wish for because wishes carry power, create energy, and affect change" and, they just might come true. And many times I have heard "every action has a reaction or consequence" and we "reap what we have sown."

With this rudimentary knowledge of the laws of nature, you can now more consciously tap into the enormous power of the universe, channeling it into your pagan practice, your magic and your life. You can use the universal energy in a focused, fantastic, and transformative way, to create abundance and gratitude within your life.

If energy is never destroyed but can change form, what could you do with all the energy currently spent worrying? Can you transform yourself, refocusing on abundance and gratitude?

Enlightened Transformation

Let's put the laws of nature to work in our lives, using their structure as a basis for transformation. Starting with the heavy energy of worry, use the Law of Polarity to turn it around. Write a short list specifically identifying what you are worrying about. Now turn it around, literally, and identify the opposite of what your worry is about and write it in a second column. These opposites will be the basis of your visualization. Envision in great detail what you want to be your reality. See it, know it, experience it, and feed your energy into it, knowing that the laws of growth, the laws of polarity, and the laws of cause and effect work with you to shift the universe. Use this transformative technique daily to amplify positivity, light and abundance.

An old platitude says: Gratitude is an attitude. And because mental energy can be made manifest into physical form, it is possible to use affirmation, intention, and meditation to create a positive polarity, attracting more good energy to us. Make a list of the good things in your life by doing a daily gratitude list. Each day identify ten things that you are grateful for. Do it quickly, without too much thought. Express your gratitude for small things and enormous things. Just write it down: Today I am grateful for ____ in my life. It might be "my cats," or "the good breakfast of fresh fruit I ate," or "the Sun shining." There are many things to be grateful for in each and every day.

Practicing gratitude will shift your perception, focusing you on the positive abundance that surrounds you. As your perception shifts, you energetically charge yourself, and through the law of attraction bring more goodness to you.

Purposefully cultivating good energy is easy. Start small and let it build. Learn to appreciate the beauty and joy that endlessly surround us. Notice the magnificence of nature and the colors of the changing sky. Laugh with children and throw sticks for dogs. The more we shift our focus to beauty, joy, and pleasure, the more their energy increases in our lives. The same is true of monetary wealth and abundance. "Find a penny, pick it up, all day long you will have good luck." Thank the Goddess for her blessings, and welcome her abundance in every form. Affirm daily that She provides for you.

When we put such simple practices into daily action, we cultivate a cloak of positive energy around us, create a positive charge within ourselves that attracts positive energy. With goodness surrounding us, we can feel abundant without having to buy or consume. With an internal source of abundance we are less swayed by the advertising that tells us we need to have things, so we can do and be better, are wrong.

Be, Do, and then Have

Advertising would have us believe that we need to have things in order to do more of what we want to do, and then we will be happy. But judging by the Laws of Nature, that is the reverse of the truth. Advertisers have the "be, do, have" paradigm backward. If everything is made of energy, then we are pure energy. The realm in which we have the most influence is within ourselves so we must start there, with the being. To be happy, we must think happy, act happy, cultivate happy, and attract happy. And then, charged with happiness on an energetic level, we will have happiness.

In order to be happy, or successful, or wealthy, we must first focus on being that energy that we are trying to attract to our lives. When our own well-being and happiness are the center of our focus, the rest of our life changes. By enjoying restorative sleep, nutritious food, joyous exercise and loving relationships, we cultivate essential joy, goodness, and satisfaction at our core. As this energy builds, it radiates out, attracting more like-minded energy. When we take time for quiet contemplative practices, for magical and spiritual work, we become more in sync with the universe and present in the moment.

So be happy and healthy, satisfy your own personal needs. Make these your priority, and don't think of it as selfish. When you generate good energy, you attract good energy, emit good energy, and radiate good energy. And this affects everyone and anything you come into contact with. Around you, people will feel the cumulative effects of your positive energy.

There is nothing wrong with being, doing, and having so long as they are in the proper perspective and natural order.

And with your newfound abundance of good energy, you have extra to devote to doing things for others. We can easily do good things for our partners, children, families, and our communities.

You can also use your abundant good energy to do things for money, like work. Miraculously, the energy we invest into being creates an abundance that allows us to do, and this can provide us with money, which is stored energy. Money can buy us things and facilitate having. Seen through the lens of the laws of nature, having is a natural result of first being and then doing.

There is nothing wrong with being, doing, and having so long as they are in the proper perspective and natural order. When we cultivate a lifestyle that is focused on simple joy and happiness, we invest in the larger cycle that provides for all our needs, and that aligns us with the magical energy and good works of the Goddess nature.

By aligning your consumerism with your spiritual beliefs, and basing it on the laws of nature, you can transform yourself, lightening your debt load . . .

But without the parameters of the laws of nature to guide us, we fall into the trap of seeking to have without being or doing. And this can create a vacuum of negative energy, one that can suck us down into worry, despair, emptiness, and bankruptcy. Whether it is having a home, having contentment, or having loving relationships, having only occurs as a result of first being, and then doing. Remember that money is stored energy, and if you haven't generated good energy being good and doing good things, then no good will come of having.

Live Lightly

By seeking personal well-being and happiness as the root of our spiritual practice, we choose to live within our means, and live lightly on the earth. When our fulfillment comes from the cultivation of good energy within and around us, not from the collection of things that we can acquire, we experience the lightness of being associated with fulfillment and joy.

Aligned with the laws of nature, we work with and through the greater good. We are in touch with the universal flow of energy. As

we practice cultivating positive energy, our focus turns to deeper spiritual fulfillment in life and with this come enlightenment. Rather than trying to fill meaninglessness and emptiness with consumer goods, we can turn within to create joy, peace, and contentment through a focus on our essential selves—energy and light.

And as we are able to see the world we live in as a universe composed of energy, in which we have transformative and creative power, we are drawn to making consumer choices in line with out beliefs and spiritual/magical practices. Making the direct connection between our spiritual beliefs and consumer practices, we can start to make buying decisions in line with our pagan values, and direct our energy into things we truly believe in when we exercise our purchasing power.

Whether you turn to voluntary simplicity, scaling down your consumerism to include only basic human needs, or whether you choose to more consciously use your money to invest in your beliefs through fair trade purchases, consuming locally or buying secondhand, you have the power to transform your own consumer habits, and the energy that both feeds into it and results from it. By aligning your consumerism with your spiritual beliefs, and basing it on the laws of nature, you can transform yourself, lightening your debt load, enlightening yourself, and living lightly on the pagan path.

RESOURCES

One of my favorite books is *Creative Visualization* by Shakti Gawain. She doesn't fully outline the laws of nature but provides lots of focused information on using visualization to shift energy and change your reality.

There are also lots of great books out there about voluntary simplicity—simplifying your life and clearing out the clutter. Many of these are written by Elaine St. James. Check out *Simplify Your Life*, which is a culmination of years of trying to simplify her own life and what she learned on the way. She also wrote *Inner Simplicity*, which addresses more matters of a spiritual nature, encouraging the reader to let go of "stuff" to make room in their homes and lives for deeper spiritual satisfaction.

Some great Web sites include: http://www.newdream.org, the Web site of the Center for a New American Dream, which is exactly what its name implies. The site urges consumers to think about what they buy, how they consume, and what the real effects and hidden costs are of consumption. Another site, http://www.simple-living.net, is chock full of ideas and resources for anyone interested in intentional simplicity, and http://www.pathtofreedom.com is a Web site devoted to providing and teaching the tools, skills, and ways to live a self-sufficient lifestyle.

As you strive to live lightly on the pagan path, remember to let the laws of nature rule. "What you feed, grows," so plant the seeds of joy and positivity, nurture them, and see them grow radiantly light!

Dallas Jennifer Cobb *lives an enchanted life in a waterfront village in Canada. Forever scheming novel ways to pay the bills, she's freed up resources for what she loves most: family, gardens, fitness, and fabulous food. When she's not running on country roads or wandering the beach, she's writing and daydreaming.*

Illustrations: Neil Brigham

The Divine and Me

Gede Parma

I was quite young, about five years old, when I turned to my mother in the temple grounds in my father's village, pointed to an elderly man amidst the chaotic throng of people, and asked quite avidly, "Is that God?"

It was later explained to me that the man in question was indeed a holy man who had come to my father's village in the mountains for the ceremony. However, most of the time the holy man held his hermitage in the jungle, without eating or drinking for months, even years, on end. Abstaining from those things we humans know are necessary for our

livelihoods was common practice for this particular spiritual master, and indeed it worked for him.

In my innocence, viewed through the eyes of a child, I saw God in this man. I saw the presence of the Divine. Now in my twentieth year, this is crystallized for me in the fact that I am a pagan priest, a witch, a follower of the Old Ways of the Earth. My relationship to and perception of the Divine have evolved in my short time in this incarnation, however my views tend to become more inclusive as I grow older and wiser.

What is the Divine? Why is it important? These are questions commonly asked by practitioners of spirituality, and I will endeavor to answer them here. The Divine is the all-encompassing, all-pervasive, quintessence that dwells in all things—it is the animating force of Life that suspends the Continuum. Why is this important? To that I shall answer with a further question—why is it not? And what is the difference?

When I first began to consciously unravel the threads of my spiritual tapestry, I chose to identify as a Wiccan because in those early years most of what I read seemed to suggest that Wicca was synonymous with witchcraft. I wanted so much to be a part of a magickal tradition that I simply went with whatever jumped at me first. Wicca, being the foremost neopagan tradition, was the obvious choice. So, as zealous neophytes do, I took on the mantle of the Wiccan and began to cast circles, call quarters, and invoke the God and the Goddess. Who this god and goddess were exactly, I hadn't quite worked out. I did know, however, that they were inextricably linked and a part of each other—a supernal mother/father couple (a European yin-yang, perhaps?). I did not know at the time that these names (albeit titles of convenience) derived from Gardnerian labels for their two deities who have secret, oath-bound names and are definitely beings unto themselves—a triple goddess of the Moon and Fate, and a horned god of hunting, death, and resurrection. This knowledge is not afforded to those practitioners of eclectic Wicca early on in their journeys (as the traditional training is amiss). A generic all-mother and all-father became the norm in what is often called neo-Wicca. I grew to be deeply dissatisfied with this notion. In my experience, there was more to nature and to life than the parental duo. I saw amazing, vivid colors—not just black and white.

After struggling for four or so years with this particular ditheistic concept, I began to receive visions from the Roman goddess Fortuna, and I excitedly embraced her. It felt strange, and theologically insane (at least from the Wiccan point of view) to be invoking the God and the Goddess, and then Fortuna. I simply could not believe in my heart that the Goddess was all goddesses and the God was all gods—I do not subscribe to Dion Fortune's theology.

Eventually, I conducted an "aspecting" ritual in which, for a month, the goddess Fortuna would dwell with me and imbue me with her best qualities. The most interesting thing to come out of this experience was the symbol that Fortuna kept revealing in my visions.

The symbol was an equilateral triangle with a dent in one side. I realized that ironically, the triangle (point up) is a common symbol of spirituality—especially when that spirituality emphasizes Deity as the focus.

Fortuna was trying to tell me that it was time for me to sort out my "kinks"—to affirm my focus. Also, the Goddess wanted me to know that no matter what path I chose it would be the right one for me, as whichever way the triangle points, it is still the same triangle. Fortuna's presence in my life gradually diminished until once more I was left with a void. Then everything changed.

In the spring of 2004, a goddess came into my life and shook the very core of my being. She came swiftly, and yet she lingered in shadow for some time before I allowed myself to embrace her. It was the Full Moon when I first met her. I was in circle invoking the Goddess (the generic neo-Wiccan idea) when I looked up to the kitchen window and saw an ethereal outline of a woman directly in front of me. My body prickled with gooseflesh as I took in the vision, and I whispered softly, "Persephone."

As my relationship with Persephone deepened, a thread of synchronicity began to weave its way through my life. More deities from the Greek pantheon began to appear to me, and I began to honor them regularly. I even adopted ritualistic practices from Hellenismos (reconstructed Greek paganism) in order to open myself more directly to their power current. I completely embraced my once-hidden polytheism. I was reliving the wonder of my youth, as I was raised in Hinduism, which boasts one of the most colorful pantheons in the world. I approached each deity and being as an individual—affording them the same respect and consideration that I would any physical being.

When I moved to Brisbane, the capital city of my state, in 2006, I found myself sharing house space with two amazing witches who were very much aware of their Celtic ancestry and its significance in their spirituality. I have always been one to wait to be contacted first rather than to independently adopt or appropriate a deity, being, or custom as my own. I was very much aware of my Celtic-Irish ancestry (my mother's side), but it was only after meeting these two wonderful people and the experiences that ensued that I finally met with the raw and undeniable presence of the ancient Tuatha. Around the same time, I began to explore my connection with the wild magick of the Fey, and I co-founded the Coven of the WildWood, which is now the mother coven and formulator of the modern WildWood tradition.

If I exist physically (or mentally, emotionally, etc.) in this space, and you exist physically in the space you happen to inhabit, what truly distinguishes "there" from "here?"

After a year and a day of dedication in the inner court of the coven, I traveled to a beautiful hinterland mountain for my initiation. It was there that I swore eternal service to the sacred four of my coven—the Weaver, the Green Man, the Crescent-crowned Goddess,

and the Stag-horned God. I became a priest of my tradition, of the realm/current it represented, and the forces that inspired it. Later that year, Aphrodite came to me and took me as hers in a moving, spontaneous drawing down.

Beyond all this, and within it too, is the Force (that thing) that I call the Great Mystery.

The Great Mystery

Here I am there; there you are. What is the difference? If I exist physically (or mentally, emotionally, etc.) in this space, and you exist physically in the space you happen to inhabit, what truly distinguishes "there" from "here?" Is it perception, the constant factor of personal experience (i.e., you!) or is there a physical delineation between these spatial 'co-ordinates'? Quantum theory would suggest that there is no separation between anything. All matter is, at its foundation, a quivering mass of subatomic particles joined by . . . what? Black matter? The Great Mystery. It's not an answer, and it's not a question. It's that thing in between and on either side. It is a question that does not require resolution; an answer with no question. It's there. It's the source of the fifth element—Spirit. I often call Spirit the providence of the Great Mystery.

Theological debate on the nature of the Divine has been raging for centuries. The general monotheistic tendency is to declare the total omnipotence of God (the one and only), and hard polytheists protect the rights of deities as individuals. There are the Wiccan di-theists who believe in the God and the Goddess, and that all male deities are facets of the God and all female deities are facets of the Goddess. However, to this I say, "don't abuse me with your gender politics," (in jest of course!). Simply put, I tend to look beyond dualities of any kind. I understand the significance and usefulness of the idea. It's just not for me.

As a witch and initiated priest, it is part of what I do to think on and ponder these mysteries of life.

The point of journeying is to evolve, though no one ever truly realizes these changes until one stops and reflects on what has gone and what will be. To stand in the present, on the threshold of summation and potential, is to actualize those subtle, inner-changes that have occurred on a deeper level.

As I write this, I am aware of so much. I would even go so far as to say that in this moment—right now—I am utterly connected to the

Infinite. I am conscious that I am divine and that everything that is apparent and those things that are unseen are also of the same.

Once upon a time the idea of God was irrelevant to me. When I was young and Lucy the dog would run away, I would kneel at our home altar, light the candles and incense, and pray to Lord Ganesh for Lucy's safe return. In every case she did return. There was never a doubt in my mind that this amazing universe is populated by divine beings. I felt the undying radiance of it in my heart, in my life, in nature, and in love. I didn't live in a reality that denied color. I was never encouraged to place faith or bind myself to moralistic dualities. In fact, the only spiritual advice my mother ever gave me was to treat others as I would have them treat me. The choice to give reverence to the Divine was my own. The gods were there though, and they always have been.

. . . .

As a witch and initiated priest, it is part of what I do to think on and ponder these mysteries of life. The pondering has no purpose of its own. It simply allows for the possibility of an expansion of consciousness. Exploration and adventure are healthy ways to make contact with parts of the Self and the universe that have previously remained untapped. In my experience the gods encourage the pondering—they revel in questions. How boring would their existences be if they had no questions to feign answers for? Answers are meaningless unless they are associated or identified with a preceding question. When answers are necessary, questions become hollow and misaligned. Do you seek to know simply to know? Or is it that knowledge is an inspiration to ask another question? I feel the latter has more to offer the serious journeyer.

When faced with the question of how to relate to the Divine, I always say, "They do not care how we seem Them, only that we do." If one can look outside of himself or herself and see beauty in the world, then one can go beyond this and deepen their understanding by realizing: that which is without is also within. As the Charge of the Goddess affirms:

> And you who seek to know me,
> know that the seeking and yearning
> will avail you not,
> unless you know the Mystery:
> For if that which you seek,
> you find not within yourself,
> you will never find it without.
> For behold,
> I have been with you from the beginning,
> and I am that which is attained
> at the end of desire."

Gede Parma is an initiated priest and cofounder of the dynamic Brisbane-based Coven of the WildWood, mother coven of the WildWood Tradition of witchcraft. He blends Hellenismos with his ancestral traditions of Eire and Bali and is devoted to his Gods of Blood and of Breath. Gede is a consecrated priest to his soul-Goddess Persephone and to the Lady of Love, Aphrodite. He is a ritual-crafter, palmist, cartomancer, and clairvoyant. Gede Parma is the author of Spirited: Taking Paganism Beyond the Circle, published by Llewellyn Publications (2008). His e-mail is hiphellenicwitch@hotmail.com and his Web site is http://www.gedeparma.com/

Illustrations: Lydia Hess

My Goddess Body

Gail Wood

In ritual and magick, we call to the Goddess to join us in our bodies, hearts, and souls by saying, "By the air that is her breath, by the fire of her bright spirit, by the water that is her blood, and by the earth that is her body." With our breath, with our passionate spirits, with the blood pumping through our veins, and by the bone and sinew of our bodies, we become the Goddess in ritual and magick. We say to ourselves and to each other in powerful statements of the union of our own inner-divine with the transcendent power of

the universe: "I am Goddess." In our circles, we sing our union with the sacred world with the chant: "Earth my body, water my blood, air my breath, and fire my spirit," as we are the embodiment of divine power and the elements of life.

The earth we live on is an enormous and magnificent place. Great oceans rise and crash on beaches, small streams and ponds lap on rocky shores, enormous mountains tower above us, and the deserts shimmer with heat and delicately support mysterious wildlife. Flatlands, lowlands, highlands, cliffs, rocks, sand, and soil all support life and create beauty. Across the continents, oceans, and seas, we have enormous diversity; and we find beauty in the landscape, the animals, plants, trees, and creatures who live in and on the Earth. Despite all the destruction that humans have done to the planet, this is still a place of incredible, varied, and magnificent beauty. The Charge of the Goddess tells us that She is the beauty of the Earth, the Moon among the stars, and the mystery of the waters. When we say, "I am Goddess," we are saying we are all these things about ourselves.

But do we mean it? Do we experience jaw-dropping awe of the beauty of the Earth as we embody the sacred? Do we experience the encompassing love the Goddess feels for us as individuals and for inhabitants of this wondrous world? When we look at our bodies, do we see the fabulous multiplicity of human physical diversity? Intellectually, we understand it. Emotionally, we struggle to accept this as truth and as a gift. It is very difficult because we live in a socially structured world as well as in the beauty of the Earth. Human beings need other human beings. To be socialized means achieving balanced levels of conformity and independence in order to survive and thrive economically and socially. I would say that when we are in circle and we call the Goddess down into our bodies, we experience that joy, beauty, and astounding wonder that accompanies our connection with the boundless and divine universe. Sometimes, in our everyday life, we find echoes of that wonder. Sometimes that feeling can be elusive, leaving us with feelings of self-hatred.

It is very difficult to love our bodies in our culture. Several religions teach us that the body is the temple that houses Spirit, but it is a message that media and societal messages contradict, both overtly and subliminal. The media sends us very mixed messages about body size, health, eating, sex, pleasure, and pain—any of the experiences that cause our bodies to *feel*. The messages confuse and hurt us, and leave us no tools to accept or love our bodies. Moreover, we are taught not to trust our inner wisdom; and with others projecting their own vision of bodily perfection on to our perceptions, it's very difficult to see ourselves as beautiful. Our bodies do have wisdom and we carry all our thoughts and ideas within our physical selves. Our bodies remember, our bodies heal, and our bodies wound. We are beings of incredible power, and we often use that power to injure ourselves so deeply that recovery is difficult; so we live our lives disconnected from our own divine bodily radiance. On some level, we dampen and dim our inner divine until what is left is insatiable longing and neediness.

It doesn't matter if we are a woman or a man, if we are old or young, if we are short or tall, or if we are fat or thin, at some point in our lives most of us learn to be unhappy with our bodies. Some of us learn to hate our bodies. As a learned behavior, we can unlearn that hatred and unhappiness. It isn't easy. Intellectually we know it. There are lots of helpful psychological strategies available. We may try them and are successful when we persevere. As with everything worthwhile in life, it takes the persistence of practice. We maintain our new attitudes and understanding through regular practice.

Your body remembers every word you say about it and think about it.

Rather than imposing a stringent set of tasks, such as dieting, to create change, a practice of body acceptance helps you psychologically, emotionally, and spiritually. You can achieve what you desire through persistent, gentle, accepting practice. We have to maintain a balance between hyper-vigilance and ignoring the situation; either of these strategies blinds us to who we really are. We maintain the structure of our strategy rather than practice who we are. As people on the pagan path who work magick to create change, we have the additional ability to approach our situation with the spiritual power of the sacred.

We already have many skills in our toolkit, even though we may have a tendency to discount our abilities. We are magic. Meditations that ground us in the power of Mother Earth and connect us to the universal life force are tools for change that we can apply to loving our goddess bodies. Feeling the energy of the Earth in our bodies and knowing the magnificent beauty of the Earth empowers us with every breath should be part of our daily practice. To amplify our understanding of our divine embodiment, we can intensify our grounding meditation and call the beauty of the Earth into us.

Grounding Meditation

Choose a place that creates that sense of beauty and power when you think of it. For me that would be the beaches of the Atlantic Ocean. So in my meditations to connect to the beauty of the Earth, I go there in my meditation and gently send my roots into that place and pull the heart-stopping splendor of it into my body. When you feel that wonderful energy merge with your own energy, you dance in ecstasy of delight, power, and beauty.

As you practice merging your energy with beautiful Earth energy, you must stop the negative messages you send to your body. Your body remembers every word you say about it and think about it. Not the random thoughts that pass through your head and move on, but the words you say or think with passion or regularity. Statements like "I hate my lips," or "I'm a nail-biter," said with force or frequency are retained in our body as truth. Even statements made by others, when we believe them, get added to the lexicon of bodily knowledge. "You have your mother's nose" may have been meant lovingly and yet you retained it as an insult; it, therefore, becomes a wound within your body that does not heal. From this point forward, you **must** promise yourself that you will cease those negative messages about yourself, and when you do hear one that you will do your best to transform the message so it will do no harm to you. Change takes time and persistence, so forgive yourself if you falter. Eventually, you will replace your negative messages with messages of love and acceptance.

After learning to replace your negative self-talk with loving messages, move on to accepting the reality of the statement, "I am Goddess." For a long time, I said the words followed by the mental statement "yeah right," which my body retained as the sarcastic message: I am Goddess—yeah right. While our unconscious may not hear sarcasm, our bodies definitely do. "I am Goddess" is an affirmative statement of our divine nature, and we should proclaim it to our own true self in ways that can be embraced. One of my teachers quipped that "affirmations are lies we tell ourselves until they come true." So you can keep saying and practicing "I am Goddess," until it comes true. You can reinforce that practice with images of the Goddess in your household and daily life. You are Athena, Venus, Willendorf, Astarte, Eve, Lilith, and all the goddesses of the world. You are She. Find images that please you, surround yourself with them, and practice saying and knowing that you are Goddess. Sing goddess songs in celebration of your sacred self. Dance goddess dances in celebration of your goddess self. We need to remind ourselves daily, even hourly that we are the *embodiment* of the sacred.

There are a host of body acceptance exercises for us to add our magical power to. One of the most common is to stand in front of a mirror and take a body inventory. The most effective way is to be nude in front of a full-length mirror. You go from the feet up and look at each body part in as much detail as possible and state: what it is and what it does, how it feel, and how well it does or does not serve its purpose, and then how you feel about it. When doing this exercise by yourself, recording what you say will help you understand yourself better when you listen to the playback. This exercise is a powerful psychological and emotional tool because you get to

look at your body in terms of its functionality and also in terms of how you feel about it in an honest and nonthreatening environment. When you are done, you will have a good sense of how you feel, the messages you send to and about your body, and a pathway to change.

Working with a powerful process does not make it an easy one, so instant body acceptance is not the goal; we need to understand that this becomes a first step on a journey of many steps. It gets easier with repetition. This exercise reveals things to your conscious mind, feelings you may have kept hidden. To add a spiritual component, you may want to do this in ritual space, either simple or complex. Begin and end each statement by thanking the goddess for the body part and for your feelings about it. Once you have some ideas on what you want to change about your attitude about your body, you can add them to your ritual and spellwork.

As we work in detail to change our attitudes and changing the things we don't like about ourselves, it is easy to get immersed in our failures and lose site of the big vision. The big vision is that our body is sacred, elemental, and divine, just as surely as the wonderful landscapes of this glorious world. We are blood, bone, skin, hair, heart, and soul connected to fire, water, air, and earth, just as surely as everything else is so connected. We forget that connection in our concerns about working, paying bills, coping with all the things of everyday life. We can connect regularly to our sacred fire, earth, water, air to know we are the Goddess just as surely as is the Earth herself.

Find Your Inner Divinity Meditation

This is a meditation that takes us away from the anxiety of trying to fix things and focuses on understanding our inner sacred nature; the second half of the meditation focuses on bringing our inner divinity into the light. As active sacred beings, we can become a Goddess as we magically flip on our light switch! You can do this meditation in one sitting or do it as a series of meditations. As a general rule, this is used as part of a regular personal practice of living the magical life.

Settle yourself into a relaxed space away from all the distractions. Get in a comfortable position and relax. You might want to spend some time chanting or toning to yourself before you begin. Take a long, deep, healing and cleansing breath. Take another deep breath and let go of any distractions. Take a second deep breath and breathe in peace and harmony. And take a third deep breath and let it out with a musical tone. Hold the note and then let if fade, as the last vibrations of the tone reverberate through your body, turn your attention inward and see those vibrations as beautiful bubbles of light, swirling and twirling inside you. These beautiful bubbles of you are the energy of you. Whirling and twirling, this is the energy, the beautiful energy of you. Feel it filling you and healing you. With your focused attention, move the energy around. If there is any place that is hurting or needs some tender loving care, let the light smooth out those rough spaces. Breathe deeply and be filled with the beauty and joy of this light.

As you breathe deeply, see the lights change colors: yellow for air, red for fire, blue for water, and green for earth. Feel and see the energy move inside you, filling you with the elemental energy of each color. Feel the energy of the elements fill you and heal you. As the energy twirls and swirls inside you, notice if any of the energy bubbles are clouded or less bright. With your attention, change the color of the bubble until it is a clear, vibrant color, pulsating with the energy of life. Keep on breathing as the energy swirls inside you. Notice which elements are abundant and which are scarce. Without judgment, just observe.

Now focus your attention on air and note the yellow energy inside you. Summon your breath and use it to create more and more yellow energy inside you. As you are filled with this energy of air, feel your intellect, your imagination, and your intuition grow stronger and more present in your life. Breathe in the power of the element of air and know that you are more articulate, intuitive, and imaginative.

Now focus your attention on fire and note the red energy inside you. Summon your willpower and use it to create more and more red energy inside you. As you are filled with this energy of fire, feel your courage, your passion, and your fierceness grow stronger and more present in your life. Feel the will grow within you and know that you are more powerful, effective, and passionate.

Now focus your attention on water and note the blue energy inside you. In tune with your heartbeat, create more and more blue energy inside you. As you are filled with this energy of water, feel your soul, your emotions, and your instinct grow stronger and more present in your life. Feel the power of the element of water and know that you are more loving, compassionate, and understanding.

Now focus your attention on earth and note the green energy inside you. Summon your strength and use it to create more and more green energy inside you. As you are filled with this energy of earth, feel your connectedness, your stability, and your steadiness grow stronger and more present in your life. Breathe in the power of the element of earth and know that you are more steadfast, grounded, and strong.

With a long deep breath, watch the energies of air, fire, water, and earth dance in harmony in your body. Feel fabulous, joyful, wise, strong, grounded, and steadfast. Feel it all in your body. Feel your body. As this energy whirls, feel your skin, your heart beating, your bones, your flesh, your fingers, your toes, and all of you in between. Feel the mind and spirit reside in this body of bone, blood, sinew,

and skin. Glory in the marvelous, jaw-dropping complexity of many systems working together to make you the person you are. You are the Goddess.

Now breathe deeply and settle into a calming pattern of breath. Center yourself in your heart-center, with your elemental self pooling there. Feel the glow of divinity come from your center. Feel it as a light kindled and burning and then feel it grow stronger and more powerful. Feel it move from you into the outer world and surround you in a circle. Then feel the universal energy of air, fire, water, and earth flow and move in harmony with yours. Feel the transcendent divine universe reach out and embrace you. Feel all those energies braid together and harmonize. You may feel it as music, as vibration, as silence, or as a change. Breathe deeply into that connection and sacred flow. Breathe deeply and let it flow in your body, around your body, and out into the universe. You are a child of the universe, being born each moment, just as the chant says.

When it is time, take a deep breath and return to the here and now. Take another deep breath and return to your physical place. Take another deep breath and open your eyes. Take some time to express the wisdom of this journey by writing in a journal, a poem, a drawing, or other expression.

After some time, you can incorporate these exercises or variations of them into a daily personal practice. As with any spiritual path, it's not about setting aside time once in awhile but in incorporating it into your life. Understanding your Goddess self and your Goddess body is something to practice every day. We make mistakes and take a step backwards and then we make great strides and move forward, but in order to live the embodiment of the Goddess we are, we must dance every step of every dance. This is not a spiritual path for wallflowers. We are in the center of the dance floor with our arms widespread, embracing our own beauty, power, rightness, and joy.

Gail Wood *started her writing career early when a story she wrote in the first grade was posted on the board by her teacher. The story was about Jo-Jo the monkey. Her mother saved that story for Gail! She is the author of* Rituals of the Dark Moon: 13 Rites for a Magical Path *published by Llewellyn in 2001. Currently, she lives in a 100+ year-old house with her partner Mike and their two dogs. Mike shares her spiritual interests and is an exceptionally fine priest, following the ecstatic path of Gaia.*

Illustrations: Kathleen Edwards

Mystical Lineage: Initiation as Transformation

Elizabeth Barrette

All human cultures recognize the concept of lineage, the genetic and social connections between people in the same family. Families take different shapes in different cultures—sometimes even within cultures—but we still recognize that common bond of ancestors, age-mates, and descendants. Some religious and magical traditions also acknowledge a type of lineage. This mystical lineage concerns the bond between teacher and student or the bond between a group and its initiates. In this way, knowledge and customs pass down from founders or other important people to their students, and then to others. This transmission of material can make profound changes in people.

Transformation is the crucial threshold in a long process of growth: a point of radical change. Initiation is the point at which someone becomes a member of a mystical lineage. The goal of transformation belongs to many traditions. Historical alchemists describe several stages of alchemical transformation. Buddhists strive for enlightenment. Whatever the name, these experiences remain variations on a theme. But what *is* transformation?

A person who has not invested in inner growth exists only as a body, mind, and spirit. The body tends to rule the mind, and the mind has little connection to the spiritual plane. Yet the more we study the paths of the soul, the more changes we go through, learning along the way those tricks the body uses to distract us. Gradually, we discover how to glean out the important information without letting our base nature get the better of us and the mind gains ascendance over the body.

From that quiet state, the mind becomes more aware of the spiritual energies and planes of reality. With practice (and especially meditation) our ability to tune in to our higher selves, the Divine, and the universe—however you conceive of That Which Lies Beyond—increases. Then spirit properly rules over mind, which rules the body, and it becomes possible to live in peace and grace because all our parts are working together rather than at cross purposes.

At certain points in this journey, the gradual discovery and change tends to take a leap forward, and we have one of those "Aha!" moments in which everything abruptly makes sense. These are points of transformation. Magical-spiritual traditions create maps for people to follow in their quest for growth, including bridges of initiation. With the education already provided by a mentor and the group at large, an initiate is primed for transformation at the point

of initiation. This provides a safe context and support for what can sometimes be a disconcerting change.

Mystical lineage affects the contemporary pagan community in diverse ways.

A key feature of any magical-spiritual tradition is whether or not lineage is considered important. Some traditions do, some don't. Mystical lineage customarily depends on some kind of formal adoption into the tradition. This can manifest as initiation, attunement, or another ceremony; in this article, "initiation" refers to any such ceremony. Initiation serves multiple purposes. Different traditions may therefore emphasize a different combination of these.

One purpose for initiation is containment. Some knowledge and customs are to be kept private for initiates only. Mainstream religions do this, too. The Catholic Church, for example, sets rules about who may receive Holy Communion. Other information is just plain dangerous in the wrong hands, and certain techniques require training to perform safely. By requiring a commitment before teaching such things, the members of a tradition can reduce the chance of inappropriate distribution of their secrets. Nothing can contain it altogether, though, as evidenced by all the "secret teachings" books on the shelves today!

Closely related in purpose to containment is education. A tradition can be passed on only by when it is taught to other people. Incoming members must learn the particular beliefs and practices of their new tradition, which takes time. Gardnerians, in particular, are supposed to copy the entire contents of their mentor's Book of Shadows, so that all Gardnerians share, at least, the core liturgy. Those of close lineal relation, such as trainees of the same high priestess, may have almost identical books. The initiation forms a vital part of this whole learning process.

Thus, the initiation itself becomes a goal to strive toward. It is also a reward for investing the time and energy to learn about the tradition and for making the commitment to join. Finally, the initiation marks a milestone in a person's progress, the culmination of their studies and efforts. This tends to be a powerful transformative experience.

Lineage in Traditions

A key feature of any magical-spiritual tradition is whether or not lineage is considered important. Some traditions do, some don't, and this can start serious arguments. Many groups revere lineage and look down on groups that don't or on solitaries who practice outside the group context. The attitude: If you haven't been initiated into a coven by someone with proper lineage, then you're not a real witch, can hurt people's feelings. There is no one *true, right, and only way*. Rather, there is a multitude of ways, so respect other people's right to choose their path as you have chosen yours.

Among pagans, Wicca is one of the most recognized traditions. Wicca's roots go back at least as far as Gerald Gardner, who is considered by many to be the father of Wicca. Gardner claimed that it went back much further, and many people believe this, in whole or in part. Contemporary Wicca includes several branches, but Gardnerian Wicca is dominant, and all "properly initiated" witches in those traditions have a chain of people leading back to Gardner.

Western ceremonial magicians have formed various organizations. Some are more secretive than others, but most are structured enough to keep an eye on lineage. Some of the orders are themselves related. For example, the Hermetic Order of the Golden Dawn inspired the subsequent Order of Argenteum Astrum founded by Alexander Crowley. A later version is the New Reformed Orthodox Order of the Golden Dawn, a neopagan tradition with both spiritual and magical aspects drawn from earlier orders.

Another tradition famous for its use of lineage is reiki. Their lineage is created when a reiki master performs "attunements" for a student. Founded by Dr. Mikao Usui, reiki fosters a connection between the practitioner and the divine energy of the universe. The Japanese branches of reiki focus more on intuition and spirituality, while Western branches focus more on practicality and healing, but they share the same roots and many similarities that overlap. Some reiki masters have become famous for certain techniques, a particular flavor of energy, or specialization in treating particular complaints. They attract students who wish to learn that unique approach. So, each student's experience of reiki is influenced by all the masters between their teacher and Dr. Usui.

Initiatory Activities

Initiation rituals vary from one tradition to another, but common motifs emerge. These draw their power from archetypes, symbols, and deep psychological processes—many of which transcend the boundaries of culture. The techniques of initiation are themselves often part of a tradition's secret teachings.

The heart of initiation is the transition from the unknown to the known, from not knowing to knowing; and, more fundamentally, from merely knowing to *understanding*. Shortly before, during, or right after initiation are customary times for revealing crucial information to the initiate. The mentor may offer their own Book of

Shadows or other documents for the initiate to copy for personal use. The initiate may also be required to memorize their mystical lineage, so it can be recited when needed as a magical credential. Reciting the lineage aloud during initiation also helps bond the new member to the group.

The ritual designers may symbolize this process in various ways. Some traditions use the same initiation ritual for everyone, while others customize it to create a uniquely personal experience for each individual. One common motif is darkness and illumination. A group might represent this by blindfolding the initiate, leading him into a brightly lit room, and removing the blindfold. Another group might instead have the initiate kneel in a dark place, and then light candles or a bonfire.

The theme of bondage and freedom also appears. In addition to the blindfold, some initiations involve binding the wrists or making a cord that ties around the person's waist. Interestingly, the order can go in either direction: with the initiate entering freely and then "bound" to the group or entering bound and "freed" of their former limitations by the enlightening knowledge received.

Impressionable States

In order to make an initiation deeply meaningful for participants, it must create an altered state of consciousness for the initiate. Certain experiences can shift people into "imprint vulnerability," in which whatever happens will leave a lasting impression. Many techniques for achieving this state appear in traditional ceremonies around the world.

Some techniques push the body's limitations to free the mind. Sleep deprivation and fasting create a dreamy, giddy state. While these rituals are more popular in Native American or East Indian traditions than in neopaganism, some people find them very appealing.

Another family of techniques is based on sensory deprivation: periods of silence, darkness, wrapping the initiate in a blanket, and so on. These block out external distractions and encourage introspection. A third group of techniques relies on repetition to quiet the busy mind: gazing patterns, chanting, monotonous activity, and so forth, have a hypnotic effect that eventually lulls the initiate into a receptive state. Most of these require that the initiate trust the mentor to handle the process safely, but given that, they create greater opportunities than a shallower ritual performed at ordinary levels of consciousness.

In a magical tradition, the acceptable techniques are often listed in a Book of Shadows or other guide. People who have gone through the same process feel a shared bond; people who use the same techniques to achieve a state of imprint vulnerability are likely to acquire closely matching imprints. This creates a very real similarity or kinship on a psychological level—much the same way that genetics create our physical lineage. So initiation plays a vital role in taking mystical lineage from idea to reality.

Solitaries

Many pagans practice as solitaries outside of an organized group. They may do so by choice because they prefer to practice alone; or by chance if they haven't found a compatible coven in their area. What, then, does mystical lineage mean to them?

First, consider that everyone has influences on their magical and spiritual practices. The books you read and the people you talk with give you ideas about what to do (or avoid doing). Gardnerian Wicca, in particular, inspired much of the modern pagan movement, so the branches from those roots cast a wide shadow indeed.

Second, the solitary's core stance has a big impact. A solitary by chance may be seeking a group to join, which could be one that establishes mystical lineage. Conversely, a solitary by choice may

consider mystical lineage unimportant or even counterproductive. Some have had negative experiences with traditionalists who say that solitaries are not real witches because they have not been initiated into a group and, thus, have no mystical lineage.

Solitaries often choose some kind of self-initiation or dedication ceremony to mark their commitment to their personal path. For them, it is enough that they have made their choice, and perhaps that their patron deity has chosen them. Such ceremonies may have similar techniques and effects as group initiation, but there are important differences. Since you're planning the whole thing, you have only yourself to please—but you lose the exciting element of surprise. You can play to your own strengths, but you can't draw on those of other people. You don't have to worry about someone else arriving late or otherwise causing complications, but you have little or no backup if something goes wrong. Therefore, solitary ceremonies tend toward simpler design than group initiations. When planning one on your own, maximize things you do well and minimize opportunities for misfires; stick to the safer techniques.

Initiation creates an opportunity for group bonding and personal transformation. Through the use of psychological and mystical techniques, it helps the initiate achieve an impressionable state of consciousness. This is the mystical equivalent of the DNA that creates our physical lineage. Although some people quarrel over the legitimacy of mystical lineage, it is better used as common ground, for in the end, everything comes from the same Source.

Resources

"Branches of Wicca," no author listed. Retrieved from http://www.pagans.org/wicca/branches/branches.html/ 1995, 1997.

Bado-Fralick, Nikki. *Coming to the Edge of the Circle: A Wiccan Initiation Ritual.* An American Academy of Religion Book, 2005.

Grimassi, Raven. *Crafting Wiccan Traditions: Creating a Foundation for Your Spiritual Beliefs & Practices.* Woodbury, MN: Llewellyn Publications, 2008.

Astri, Ordo. "The Lineage of Ordo Astri, " Retrieved July 30, 2008 from http://www.ordoastri.org/lineage.htm/

"New Reformed Orthodox Order of the Golden Dawn," (No author) Retrieved August 7, 2008, from http://www.nroogd.org/

IO, Frater. "The Open Source Order of the Golden Dawn" October, 2003. Retrieved online at http://www.osogd.org/library/biscuits/lineage.html/

Mellowship, Dawn. "Reiki: The Way of the Universe." The Healing Co., 2005. Retrieved from online at http://www.thehealingco .com/faq's.htm/

Eliade, Mircea. *Rites and Symbols of Initiation: The Mysteries of Birth and Rebirth.* Spring Publications, 1994.

"Transformation and the Second Initiation." (No author) Diamond Light, 1999, No. 2. Retrieved online from http://www.aquaac .org/dl/99nl2art2.html/

Beyerl, Paul V. *A Wiccan Bardo, Revisited: Initiation and Self-Transformation.* Hermits Grove, 1999.

Elizabeth Barrette *has been involved with the pagan community for more than twenty years, including the study of comparative religions and interfaith work. She serves as the Dean of Studies at the Grey School of Wizardry (http://www.greyschool.com). Her book* Composing Magic *explains how to write spells, rituals, and other pagan material. She lives in central Illinois and enjoys herbal landscaping and gardening for wildlife. She has done much networking with pagans in her area, including coffeehouse meetings and open sabbats. Her other writing fields include speculative fiction and gender studies. Visit her LiveJournal "The Wordsmith's Forge" at: http://ysabetwordsmith.livejournal.com, and her homepage at http://www.worthlink .net/~ysabet/sitemap.html/*

Illustrations: Paul Hoffman

The Modern Eclectic Coven

Deborah Blake

Modern witchcraft may have its roots deep in ancient times, but the religion we practice today is actually a very young creation, still growing and changing with every passing year. Because of this, the modern coven often bears very little resemblance to the circles in which witches gathered as recently as ten or twenty years ago.

This gives rise to a number of questions, and the answers will affect the shape of witchcraft in the years to come. As covens transform to adapt to the shifting needs of today's witches, what has changed, and what has stayed the same? What does the modern witch want in a coven? What are the benefits and drawbacks of being a group witch? Where are we headed from here, and will these changes be good for the magickal community and the individual witch?

What do we mean when we talk about a coven? Historically, a coven was said to have been made up of thirteen witches, who met in secret to practice the Craft. Unfortunately, this need for secrecy means that we know very little of the makeup and methods of traditional covens, and much of what we do know tends to be inaccurate, unsubstantiated, and much debated over.

Because of this, when we talk about the traditional coven, we are usually referring to the type of group formed by Gerald Gardner, who originated modern Wicca, as well as those who followed him, such as Alex Sanders (Alexandrian Wicca), Janet and Stewart Farrar, and Raymond Buckland.

These traditional covens vary somewhat in their rules and practices, but they all tend to follow these general guidelines:

- The coven is led by a high priest and a high priestess.

- The coven follows a three-tiered degree system, involving differing levels of learning and commitment to the Craft. First-degree initiates are usually called "priest" or "witch" of the Goddess, second-degree initiates are called "magus" or "witch queen," and third-degree initiates carry the title of "high priest" or "high priestess." There is also sometimes a "maiden" who acts as assistant to the high priestess, and a "summoner" or "guardian" who acts as assistant to the high priest.

- The coven practices are often complicated and dictated by specific rules that must be adhered to strictly and very ceremoniously. A high priest and high priestess are often approached

in a formal and respectful manner, with those lower in degree kissing their hands or their feet.

- The coven members often use practices such as scourging (symbolic beating with a scourge, or whip), binding, and blindfolding to demonstrate subservience to the coven elders and a willingness to trust blindly.

- Rituals are usually done skyclad (naked) or in ceremonial robes.

- Advanced initiation may be accompanied by The Great Rite, an act of ritual lovemaking, which is always heterosexual—that is to say, the high priest would initiate a female covener or the high priestess would initiate a male covener.

- Once group members achieve the rank of high priest or high priestess (third degree) they may leave and form their own group, an act known as "hiving off."

- Rituals tools include the athame, a wand and/or staff, a cauldron, a witch's garter (a scarlet cord), a pentacle, a scourge, and a Book of Shadows that contains the rituals belonging to that coven.

- The coven activities are kept a strict secret, and outsiders are rarely if ever allowed to attend a ritual.

- The coven will usually meet for New Moons, Full Moons, and the eight sabbats of the Wiccan Wheel of the Year, as well as dedication ceremonies and the like.

- The coven will be made up of thirteen members, if possible, but numbers may vary.

- Worship is dedicated to both the God and the Goddess.

The modern coven, on the other hand, is a little harder to pin down, because it can vary widely from group to group. For instance, Dianic witches only allow women in their covens, and they worship the Goddess in her many forms (and not the God). Some groups focus on a particular culture, and the pantheon of gods that goes with it, such as Celtic or Egyptian gods. Those covens will bear very little resemblance to covens that emphasis a different culture. This is one of the reasons that many modern covens are referred to as "eclectic," since they tend to be as idiosyncratic and diverse as the multiple thousands of individual witches who have been drawn to neopaganism over the last twenty or so years.

There are some traits that most modern covens share, however, even if only in contrast to the more traditional coven:

- They are often led by only a high priestess, although they may still have both high priestess and high priest or just a high priest. Some modern covens have no leader at all, with the responsibilities shared among the members of the group or taken in turn.

- There is usually no degree system, although, again, that can vary widely. Many groups have simply the person or persons who lead (often in a fairly egalitarian manner) and everybody else. Some groups have an inner circle and an outer circle to allow for the differing amounts of experience and dedication. This may involve a "year and a day" of study to move from outer to inner level of the group.

- Coven practices may be quite simple, although many still cast a formal circle, call the quarters, and invoke the god and goddess.

- Few modern covens use the scourge or other old-fashioned tools, and many of them no longer insist on secrecy (except for whatever is necessary to protect their members who are still in the broom closet).

- Rituals are usually performed clad, although many witches still wear some kind of garb that they keep for ceremonial use only (and maybe the occasional Renaissance Faire).

- Ritual sex had been replaced by the symbolic act of placing an athame in a chalice during cakes and ale or done away with altogether.

- Modern covens are less likely to be completely heterosexual in orientation, depending upon the needs and inclinations of the members.

- The ritual tools remain much the same, with the exception of a few that are rarely used in modern covens, such as the scourge and the garter.

- Covens usually meet for New Moons, Full Moons, and the eight sabbats.

- They often put little importance on the number of people in the group, and it may be made up of as few as three members or as many as twenty.

- Most groups worship both goddess and god, but as previously stated, there are some that are dedicated to the goddess alone.

As you can see from these lists, the primary difference between the traditional coven and the modern coven is the degree of formality and the adherence to strict rules and organization. Many of the basic practices, such as creating sacred space for ritual, are still the same, although the methods used may be somewhat different.

The biggest change is that today's eclectic coven is often truly that—eclectic. My coven, Blue Moon Circle, for instance, is made up of women who come from very different magickal backgrounds. There are only one or two of us who actually refer to ourselves as Wiccans, while the others are more likely to self-identify as a witch or pagan. There is some variation in the way we each view the gods and the practice of magick.

Despite our differences, however, there is much we have in common, and we have no problem working together toward our shared magickal and spiritual goals.

This is a widespread occurrence in today's pagan world. It has come about, in part, because there are now so many paths to the neo-pagan experience that it is almost impossible to find any two witches who have exactly the same beliefs and practices. In addition, there are very few areas of the country where there are so many covens available that an individual can choose a group that perfectly matches his or her own chosen path.

Instead, a green witch, a Celtic witch, and a couple of Wiccans may end up practicing together because their approaches to magick and spirituality are all relatively close.

So what does the modern witch want from a group practice? Of course, this is a pretty broad question, but in general, I believe that today's witch is looking for a group with a reasonably similar view of the God and Goddess, a magickal practice he or she can be comfortable with, and a willingness to be open to the wishes of all its members.

While there are still witches who are interested in the more formal and hierarchical, traditional covens, many of us now prefer a more free-flowing and informal approach to magick. Neither style is better or more correct. There is no right or wrong here, only what works for each group and the individuals within it.

It is important to be aware of what you want to get out of being in a coven, and what aspects of group practice you are and aren't willing to follow. For instance, if you are looking for a coven to join and you know that you wouldn't be comfortable practicing naked, make sure that the coven you are interested in doesn't have a rule about practicing skyclad. And if it is important for you to worship the God and Goddess as Isis and Osiris, don't join a coven that is based on Celtic traditions.

... a group of witches working together on a common goal can raise an incredible amount of power.

Open and honest communication is an even more important component than ever for the modern eclectic coven. In the traditional coven, there was usually a strict set of rules that each initiate was schooled in upon joining and which the high priestess and high priest enforced rigorously. Today, many groups don't have formal rules or even a handout covering group "do's" and "don'ts," which can easily lead to misunderstandings and arguments if coven members' assumptions of acceptable behavior turn out not to match.

I strongly recommend that covens take the time to establish a few basic ground rules (often called a "compact") when starting out and that each new member be informed of these rules when he or she joins. The compact would cover such issues as when and how often the group meets, whether or not regular attendance is mandatory, and what behavior is expected from members. If everyone is to take a turn providing cakes and ale or a place for the group to meet, it is better to be clear about that from the beginning.

It can be tough to keep a coven working smoothly. After all, it is made up of a group of pagans, most of whom tend to be passionate (and sometimes eccentric) individualists. Leaders can be hard to find, and some might take advantage of their positions or simply be inept at running a group. Eventually, you will probably run into conflict within the group, and sometimes that conflict may be so bad that the coven simply gives up and disbands. Like a family, your coven will probably not be perfect, no matter how much you love it.

So why choose to practice with a group at all? After all, many modern witches are solitaries, who practice their magick on their own (either through choice or because there is no group available to them). There can clearly be disadvantages to being in a group: you have to coordinate times and places, compromise when there is disagreement, and deal with the quirks of all the individuals involved.

On the other hand, there are a number of advantages to being part of a coven (besides not always having to be the one to make the cakes). For one thing, a group of witches working together on a common goal can raise an incredible amount of power. I do some pretty effective magick on my own, but when Blue Moon Circle focuses on a magickal task in unison, the end results often amaze me.

More than the magickal boost, though, is the emotional boost that comes from sharing your spiritual beliefs with others of like mind. Some of the most powerful moments I have ever felt have taken place in circle, surrounded by the love and faith of a bunch of other witches. It is because of this feeling of joyful communion that I have chosen to be a part of an eclectic coven, rather than to practice on my own.

Which brings us to the question of whether the changes we have seen are good for the magickal community or not and where we will go from here.

It can be hard letting go of traditions, especially in a young religion that is still finding its way (even one like ours with old, old roots). But I have to believe that the modern eclectic coven is a good development in our continuing pattern of growth and change. It allows for more variety and satisfies the needs of the many members of our community for whom the traditional coven is simply not a good fit.

As for where we go from here, I suspect that only the gods know for sure, but as more and more people find their way to Wicca, witchcraft, and neopaganism, I hope that we will continue to be flexible and to flow with the needs of all the members of our community, melding the old and new together in the great cauldron that is the modern eclectic coven.

RESOURCES

Greer, John Michael. *The New Encyclopedia of the Occult*. St. Paul: Llewellyn, 2003.

Harrow, Judy. *Wicca Covens: How to Start and Organize Your Own*. New York: Citadel Press, 1999.

McCoy, Edain. *The Witch's Coven: Finding or Forming Your Own Circle*. St. Paul: Llewellyn, 1997.

Deborah Blake *is a Wiccan high priestess who has been leading her current group, Blue Moon Circle, for four years. She is the author of* The Goddess is in the Details *(Llewellyn, 2009).* Circle, Coven & Grove: A Year of Magickal Practice *(Llewellyn, 2007) and* Everyday Witch A to Z: An Amusing, Inspiring & Informative Guide to the Wonderful World of Witchcraft *(Llewellyn, 2008). Deborah was also a finalist in the Pagan Fiction Award Contest and her short story, "Dead and (Mostly) Gone" can be found in the Pagan Fiction Anthology. When not writing, Deborah runs The Artisans' Guild, a cooperative shop she founded with a friend. She is also a jewelry maker, tarot reader, an ordained minister, and an intuitive energy healer. She lives in a 100-year-old farmhouse in rural upstate New York with five cats that supervise all her activities, both magickal and mundane.*

Ilustrations: Tim Foley

The Lunar Calendar

September 2009 to December 2010

SEPTEMBER

S	M	T	W	T	F	S
		1	2	3	4	5
6	7	8	9	10	11	12
13	14	15	16	17	18	19
20	21	22	23	24	25	26
27	28	29	30			

OCTOBER

S	M	T	W	T	F	S
				1	2	3
4	5	6	7	8	9	10
11	12	13	14	15	16	17
18	19	20	21	22	23	24
25	26	27	28	29	30	31

NOVEMBER

S	M	T	W	T	F	S
1	2	3	4	5	6	7
8	9	10	11	12	13	14
15	16	17	18	19	20	21
22	23	24	25	26	27	28
29	30					

DECEMBER

S	M	T	W	T	F	S
		1	2	3	4	5
6	7	8	9	10	11	12
13	14	15	16	17	18	19
20	21	22	23	24	25	26
27	28	29	30	31		

2010

JANUARY

S	M	T	W	T	F	S
					1	2
3	4	5	6	7	8	9
10	11	12	13	14	15	16
17	18	19	20	21	22	23
24	25	26	27	28	29	30
31						

FEBRUARY

S	M	T	W	T	F	S
	1	2	3	4	5	6
7	8	9	10	11	12	13
14	15	16	17	18	19	20
21	22	23	24	25	26	27
28						

MARCH

S	M	T	W	T	F	S
	1	2	3	4	5	6
7	8	9	10	11	12	13
14	15	16	17	18	19	20
21	22	23	24	25	26	27
28	29	30	31			

APRIL

S	M	T	W	T	F	S
				1	2	3
4	5	6	7	8	9	10
11	12	13	14	15	16	17
18	19	20	21	22	23	24
25	26	27	28	29	30	

MAY

S	M	T	W	T	F	S
						1
2	3	4	5	6	7	8
9	10	11	12	13	14	15
16	17	18	19	20	21	22
23	24	25	26	27	28	29
30	31					

JUNE

S	M	T	W	T	F	S
		1	2	3	4	5
6	7	8	9	10	11	12
13	14	15	16	17	18	19
20	21	22	23	24	25	26
27	28	29	30			

JULY

S	M	T	W	T	F	S
				1	2	3
4	5	6	7	8	9	10
11	12	13	14	15	16	17
18	19	20	21	22	23	24
25	26	27	28	29	30	31

AUGUST

S	M	T	W	T	F	S
1	2	3	4	5	6	7
8	9	10	11	12	13	14
15	16	17	18	19	20	21
22	23	24	25	26	27	28
29	30	31				

SEPTEMBER

S	M	T	W	T	F	S
			1	2	3	4
5	6	7	8	9	10	11
12	13	14	15	16	17	18
19	20	21	22	23	24	25
26	27	28	29	30		

OCTOBER

S	M	T	W	T	F	S
					1	2
3	4	5	6	7	8	9
10	11	12	13	14	15	16
17	18	19	20	21	22	23
24	25	26	27	28	29	30
31						

NOVEMBER

S	M	T	W	T	F	S
	1	2	3	4	5	6
7	8	9	10	11	12	13
14	15	16	17	18	19	20
21	22	23	24	25	26	27
28	29	30				

DECEMBER

S	M	T	W	T	F	S
			1	2	3	4
5	6	7	8	9	10	11
12	13	14	15	16	17	18
19	20	21	22	23	24	25
26	27	28	29	30	31	

VIRGO

Organizing by Element

Some people have a natural knack (or obsession) for organization. Their homes look like pages from a catalog; their desks look like paragons of efficiency. But if you have trouble with clutter, try organizing by elements. For example, let's take a big stack of papers items at home. Start on a Sunday (for success) and divide the pile into four elemental piles, which you will deal with over the course of the week.

On Monday, deal with the papers relating to the element of water—anything about emotions or dreams. Put away or recycle old birthday cards and thank you notes; make art or collages from old magazines; follow up with a family member you had a dream about.

On Tuesday, tackle the fire pile. These are things relating to antagonistic relationships, like disputes with your insurer or your phone company. Deal with any lingering issues you haven't had the courage to face.

On Wednesday, blow through the air pile. In this pile you will put e-mails and letters that need to be answered, and anything relating to studying and school, such as homework, applications, even looming work projects.

On Thursday, deal with earth matters, especially your finances. Pay and file your bills, balance your checkbook, organize coupons, shred old receipts, review your 401(k). Legal papers should also be in this pile.

Elemental organizing can be applied to every area of your home and office, not just paperwork. Use Venus's romantic vibes on Friday to enjoy a luxurious bubble bath and a candlelit dinner—you deserve it!

2009
SEPTEMBER

SU	M	TU	W	TH	F	SA
		1	2	3	4 ☺ Harvest Moon, 12:02 pm	5
6	7 Labor Day	8	9	10	11	12
13	14	15	16	17	18 ● 2:44 pm	19
20	21	22 Mabon Fall Equinox	23	24	25	26
27	28	29	30			

New and Full Moon dates are shown in Eastern Time. You must adjust
the time (and date) for your time zone.

Short articles in this section by Dallas Jennifer Cobb, Elysia Gallo,
Nicole Edman, and Sharon Leah

LIBRA

Dread Full

What do you dread? What power does fear hold over you? This month, focus awareness on your biggest fears. Know what you dread, name it, and examine the power within it. Then, when the doors between the worlds swing wide at Samhain, dress up as what you dread. Maybe you fear cancer, rape, persecution, or death. Choose costumes, makeup, and symbolic items to depict your fear. For one night be what you fear. Live as what you fear. Know it. Use this newfound knowledge of the power that fear holds to overcome the fear. Take back your power, make peace with your fears. Reclaim the energy that fear once held over you, and be dread full.

SU	M	TU	W	TH	F	SA
				1	2	3
4 ☻ Blood Moon, 2:10 am	5	6	7	8	9	10
11	12 Columbus Day *(observed)*	13	14	15	16	17
18 ● 1:33 am	19	20	21	22	23	24
25	26	27	28	29	30	31

Whenever the moon and stars are set, whenever the wind is high,
All night long in the dark and wet, a man goes riding by.
Late in the night when the fires are out,
Why does he gallop and gallop about?
~Robert Lewis Stevenson

As we enter the holiday season, it can sometimes feel like a marathon—Samhain, Thanksgiving, Yule, and finally New Year's. Celebration planning, gift buying, home decorating, meal preparing . . . it's no wonder holiday stress is becoming a real and recognized problem. Here are some tips for avoiding meltdowns during this long holiday season:

Plan ahead. This seems obvious, but ten minutes spent writing a to-do or shopping list now can save you thirty minutes (and a headache) later.

Shop during off-peak times. If you can, burn a few vacation/personal hours and do your shopping on a Tuesday morning. You'll finish quicker when the grocery store or mall is empty.

Feel free to say no. People understand that the holidays are a busy time. If attending or organizing yet another party will overextend you, opt out.

Keep physically active. It's tempting to skip the gym when there's cookies to be baked, but exercise will release endorphins, burn stress, and help keep your energy level up—plus it will work off some of said cookies.

Delegate, then forget it. Find small tasks to hand over to a partner or older child, then let go of the outcome. Make sure this isn't a critical component (think cranberry sauce, not turkey), and trust that person to take care of it.

Keep it simple. Instead of shopping for, preparing, and cleaning up after a three-course meal, make that friendly get-together a potluck affair, or even just an appetizer and beverages menu.

2009
NOVEMBER

SU	M	TU	W	TH	F	SA
1 *DST ends, 2 am*	2 ☺ *Mourning Moon, 2:14 pm*	3 *Election Day (general)*	4	5	6	7
8	9	10	11 *Veterans Day*	12	13	14
15	16 ● *2:14 pm*	17	18	19	20	21
22	23	24	25	26 *Thanksgiving*	27	28
29	30					

O Lady Moon, your horns point to the East.
Shine be increased!
O Lady Moon, your horns point to the West.
Wane, be at rest.

The Laws of Magic

Do you sometimes doubt yourself or question your witchy practices? Do you feel uncertain when challenged about the validity or efficacy of magic? Don't be. Simple science, irrefutable and finite, has proven the natural laws underlying magic. The laws of physics govern magic, and echo many of the commonly held beliefs of pagans.

- What goes around comes around—energy can be changed, but not destroyed.

- Harm no one—for every action there is an equal and opposite reaction.

- You reap what you sow—like attracts like, and opposites repel.

So, when the world seems uncertain and opposing forces feel overwhelming, remember that magic is as simple as the finite laws of physics. It has been proven scientifically.

2009
DECEMBER

SU	M	TU	W	TH	F	SA
		I	2 ☺	3 ,	4	5
			Long Night's Moon, 2:30 am			
6	7	8	9	10	11	12
13	14	15	16 ●	17	18	19
			7:02 am			
20	21	22	23	24	25	26
	Yule/Winter Solstice			Christmas Eve	Christmas Day	
27	28	29	30	31 ☺		
				Long Night's Moon, 2:13 pm Lunar Eclipse New Year's Eve		

It snowed and snowed, the whole world over,
Snow swept the world from end to end.
A candle burned on the table;
A candle burned.
~Boris Pasternak, Dr. ZHIVAGO

CAPRICORN

Should auld acquaintance be forgot
and never brought to mind?
Should auld acquaintance be forgot
and days of auld lang syne?
For auld lang syne, my dear,
for auld lang syne,
we'll take a cup of kindness yet,
for auld lang syne.

~Robert Burns, AULD LANG SYNE

2010
JANUARY

SU	M	TU	W	TH	F	SA
					1 New Year's Day	2
3	4	5	6	7	8	9
10	11	12	13	14	15 ● 2:11 am Solar Eclipse	16
17	18	19	20	21	22	23
24	25	26	27	28	29	30 ☺ Cold Moon, 1:18 am
31						

All colours will agree in the dark.
~Francis Bacon

Create Your Future

Edgar Cayce taught that we have power over our future. We can plan and practice; and with intention, we can shape and create our futures. Not only can we influence our reality, but Cayce believed that our destiny influences our lived reality, energetically drawing us toward it. God, Goddess, Spirit, or Higher Power, we collaborate with the universal energy in cocreation. When we align our actions with our deepest beliefs, we grow toward our highest good.

In the darkness of winter, let the light of your desires guide you. Know that your truest desire is a manifestation of the creator's will for us. Magic is always at work in our lives, a bright spark of creativity, growing.

2010
FEBRUARY

SU	M	TU	W	TH	F	SA
	1	2	3	4	5	6
		Imbolc				
7	8	9	10	11	12	13 ●
						9:51 pm
14	15	16	17	18	19	20
Valentine's Day						
21	22	23	24	25	26	27
28 ☺						
Quickening Moon, 11:38 am						

Surely as cometh the Winter, I know
There are Spring violets under the snow.
~R. H. Newell

Practical Magic

In these final days before the Spring Equinox, we feel the pull to be free from the dark that has been winter. We watch the sun break over the eastern horizon earlier each morning, and in areas where snow has covered the ground since December, the days are warming. Melting snow drips from the eaves of our houses, tiny rivers overcome shallow ice jams and rush past driveways and along city streets, and the robins return.

We're not unlike seeds that have lain dormant all winter and which are now ready to grow toward the sun. But before we make that final push into a new solar year, it would be to our advantage to spread our roots and be nourished by our dreams, just as seeds grow a root system so they can thrive and produce a harvest in practical Virgo. For without roots, we cannot survive.

TRUST

Navigate the darkness.
Edge your way forward, one sure foot in front of the other.
Eyes closed, you trust your inner light.
Immersed in feelings you have no need of sight.
Your inner navigation knows the route.
Intuition the compass of the soul.
Feel the direction, the magnetic pull on your primal instincts.
Trust the path, trust your gut, trust your self.
Keep walking.
~Susannah Bec at http://outofmyocean.blogspot.com

2010
MARCH

SU	M	TU	W	TH	F	SA
	1	2	3	4	5	6
7	8	9	10	11	12	13
14 *DST begins,* *2 am*	15 ● 5:01 pm	16	17 *St. Patrick's Day*	18	19	20 *Ostara/* *Spring Equinox*
21	22	23	24	25	26	27
28	29 ☺ *Storm Moon,* *10:25 pm*	30	31			

Age is deformed, youth unkind,
We scorn their body, they our mind.
~Thomas Bastard

Rainy Day Spell

A childish incantation rings in my head as I step into rubber boots, pull on a heavy rain jacket, and wander outside in the cold spring rain. Observing the tender shoots of bulbs bravely poking up through the still cool soil, I know I too seek to flower, against all odds. As the sweet sap drips from the broken branch of a sugar maple tree, I know my spirit rises sweetly to meet the cycle of renewal. I breathe in oxygen—inspiration. Rain upon my face washes away the traces of winter. Divine creativity is all around.

April showers, bring May flowers,
and I am made new in the spring rain.

2010
APRIL

SU	M	TU	W	TH	F	SA
				1 *All Fools' Day*	2	3
4	5	6	7	8	9	10
11	12	13	14 ● 8:29 am	15	16	17
18	19	20	21	22 *Earth Day*	23	24
25	26	27	28 ☺ Wind Moon, 8:19 am	29	30	

I was never in love—yet the voice and shape of a woman
has haunted me these two days.
~John Keats

TAURUS

Recharge Your Batteries

In many parts of the Northern Hemisphere, this is the time of year when it finally feels like spring. Trees are budding and blossoming furiously, yards go from brown to lush green overnight, and the morning air is filled with the chattering of many varieties of birds. You can almost feel the sap surging.

Take advantage of this earthy growth period by recharging your own batteries. Go to a park or your own backyard and lie down on the grass. You might get a little muddy or damp if it rained recently so wear some suitably grungy clothes; if you plan to be outdoors for a while, don't forget to apply sunscreen beforehand.

Then, just relax. The grass might tickle, the breeze might chill, some bugs may choose to buzz you, the Sun may scorch your eyelids. Just take it all in. Breathe deeply and feel your muscles and bones seem to melt into the warm embrace of the Earth. Try to feel the world turning. Think about your place in the ecosystem, in your neighborhood, in your nation, in your continent. Feel the Earth's reawakening energies through every pore in your body, through every inch of contact with the ground. Reaffirm that you are a part of this amazing globe and let it fill you with energy.

When finished, you may wish to ground some of that energy if it is more than you need, and you may wish to say a brief thank you to the land.

SU	M	TU	W	TH	F	SA
						1 *Beltane*
2	3	4	5	6	7	8
9 *Mother's Day*	10	11	12	13 ● 9:04 pm	14	15
16	17	18	19	20	21	22
23	24	25	26	27 ☺ Flower Moon, 7:07 pm	28	29
30	31 *Memorial Day (observed)*					

Alas, that Spring should vanish with the rose!
That Youth's sweet-scented Manuscript should close!
The Nightingale that in the Branches sang,
Ah, whence, and whither flown again, who knows!
~Edward Fitzgerald

Juno's Blessing

May Juno, the mother goddess, bless you. The fighting spirit of a mother defending her offspring, Juno teaches us to fight, protecting what is sacred. Our babies—be they children, pets, works of art, or plants—need us.

Use the growing light and shorter nights of June to fuel your inner mother-goddess, battle-goddess energy. Whatever you care about, let Juno, warrior-goddess, bless it with fierce protection.

Fight for what you love. Stand up for what is right. Preserve our Mother Earth by reducing, reusing, recycling, and remembering. Be fiercely protective, loving, and strong. And be filled with the spirit of Juno when fighting for the life of our planet.

SU	M	TU	W	TH	F	SA
		I	2	3	4	5
6	7	8	9	10	11	12 ● 7:15 am
13	14 Flag Day	15	16	17	18	19
20 Father's Day	21 Litha/ Summer Solstice	22	23	24	25	26 ☺ Strong Sun Moon, 7:30 am Lunar Eclipse
27	28	29	30			

What was he doing, the great god Pan, down in the reeds by the river?
Spreading ruin and scattering ban, splashing and paddling with hoofs of a goat,
And breaking the golden lilies afloat with the dragon-fly on the river.
~Elizabeth Barrett Browning

Rain in Summer

How beautiful is the rain!
After the dust and heat,
In the broad and fiery street,
In the narrow lane,
How beautiful is the rain!
How it clatters along the roofs,
Like the tramp of hoofs
How it gushes and struggles out
From the throat of the overflowing spout!
Across the window-pane
It pours and pours;
And swift and wide,
With a muddy tide,
Like a river down the gutter roars
The rain, the welcome rain!
~Henry Wadsworth Longfellow

SU	M	TU	W	TH	F	SA
				1	2	3
4 *Independence Day*	5	6	7	8	9	10
11 ● 3:40 pm Solar Eclipse	12	13	14	15	16	17
18	19	20	21	22	23	24
25 ☺ Blessing Moon, 9:37 pm	26	27	28	29	30	31

What is fame? an empty bubble;
Gold? a transient, shining trouble.
~James Grainger, SOLITUDE

LEO

Being "August"

August, the harvest month, was the Roman month of the oracular Juno Augusta. To be *august* was to be filled with the spirit of the Goddess. Fields are filled with corn. Gardens are filled with full, fat vegetables. Orchards are heavy with fruit. As you harvest the Goddess's bounty, store some of Juno Augusta's spirit. Preserve fruit to open in the midst of winter. Make small charms of shiny stones, dried herbs, or pressed flowers to adorn your altar year round. Meditate on the light, enriching your visions with August's bright golden power. Let this harvested bounty carry you through the dark, cold times ahead, reminding you then to "be august"—filled with the spirit of the Goddess.

2010
AUGUST

SU	M	TU	W	TH	F	SA
1 Lammas	2	3	4	5	6	7
8	9 ● 11:08 pm	10	11	12	13	14
15	16	17	18	19	20	21
22	23	24 ☺ Corn Moon, 1:05 pm	25	26	27	28
29	30	31				

We have first raised a dust and then complain that we cannot see.
~Bishop Berkeley

Fall Festivals

Although autumn doesn't begin until Mabon on September 22, Labor Day weekend marks the unofficial end of summer for most folks in the Northern Hemisphere. The first Labor Day was organized by the Central Labor Union in New York City and was celebrated on September 5, 1882. That day was actually a Tuesday. The original proposal for the Labor Day celebration outlined a community parade to show the public "the strength and *esprit de corps* of the trade and labor organizations," followed by a festival for workers and their families. The day was meant to honor hardworking people and give them and their loved ones a day of rest and relaxation.

After the first Labor Day, many states began establishing a similar holiday in the following years. In 1894, the first Monday of September was made a legal federal holiday. Many countries are still on the journey to establishing workers' rights, and in recent years, Labor Day has become not only a popular weekend for last-chance family getaways, but also for activist rallies. This year, contemplate what causes resonate with you and do some research on your area's demonstration opportunities.

SU	M	TU	W	TH	F	SA
			1	2	3	4
5	6	7	8 ● 6:30 am	9	10	11
	Labor Day					
12	13	14	15	16	17	18
19	20	21	22	23 ☺ Harvest Moon, 5:17 am Mabon/ Fall Equinox	24	25
26	27	28	29	30		

O let us love our occupations,
Bless the squire and his relations,
Live upon our daily rations,
And always know our proper stations.
~Charles Dickens, THE CHIMES

LIBRA

Balance in Communication

There are times for chit-chat—you greet a coworker with an off-hand "how's it going?" Then you may move on to topics like the weather, lunch, or their new shoes. It's harmless behavior really, and it's necessary superficial conversation that keeps the wheels of society moving smoothly. Being polite helps you keep a smile on your face—even if it's sometimes a fake one—and smiles help you and others to get through the day. It happens at work, in line at the store, in interactions with servers and mechanics and hairdressers.

This communication style can be balanced by deep communication with people you really care about. When you ask your friends how they're doing, you mean it. You want to know how they're holding up against their various battles in life and when it's time to celebrate their triumphs. You want to be there to give them a bear hug when they need it and to give them your full, undivided attention. These are the people you will even turn off the TV for when they phone you. (And Goddess forbid you should try to have a deep conversation with them on the cell phone while driving!)

Wouldn't it be great if you could give a little bit of the latter style to the first group? When you run into that coworker in the hallway, or that clerk at the supermarket, or the teenager making your sandwich, could you actually look at their face and into their eyes when you ask them "how are you?" and really mean it? Instead of walking around in your own little bubble, once in a while consciously stop yourself and make an effort to burst that bubble and reach out to someone else. Listen to your intuition when it tells you to make that extra effort—you never know when someone may really need it.

OCTOBER

SU	M	TU	W	TH	F	SA
					1	2
3	4	5	6	7 ● 2:45 pm	8	9
10	11 Columbus Day (observed)	12	13	14	15	16
17	18	19	20	21	22 ☺ Blood Moon, 9:37 pm	23
24	25	26	27	28	29	30
31 Halloween/ Samhain						

Why don't you come up sometime, see me?
~Mae West, She Done Him Wrong

SCORPIO

Dark Days Decadent Brownies

As the days shorten, we remember the deep journeying within that winter encourages. Do not despair. Make these decadent brownies, and as you eat them, know the secret of darkness, which is both bitter and sweet.

When you descend to plumb the depths of your psyche during the coming dark months, bless yourself with this tasty, symbolic treat. Savor the darkness!

⅔ cup butter

5 tablespoons cocoa powder

¾ cup sugar

1 cup flour

2 eggs

1 teaspoon vanilla

1 teaspoon baking powder

½ cup walnuts or pecans, chopped

Melt butter in pan over low heat. Stir in cocoa powder. Add sugar, flour, eggs, vanilla, and baking powder. Mix well. Add nuts, and pour into greased 8 x 8 inch baking dish. Bake at 400 degrees for 15 minutes.

2010
NOVEMBER

SU	M	TU	W	TH	F	SA
	1 All Saints' Day	2 Election Day (general)	3	4	5	6 ● 12:52 am
7 DST ends, 2 am	8	9	10	11 Veterans Day	12	13
14	15	16	17	18	19	20
21 ☺ Mourning Moon, 12:27 pm	22	23	24	25 Thanksgiving Day	26	27
28	29	30				

The Duke returned from the wars today and did pleasure me in his top-boots.
~Sarah, 1st Duchess of Marlborough

SAGITTARIUS

Yule Giving

Traditional Yule gifts may include things such as an article of warm clothing, candles, a deck of cards, a tin of tea, firestarters, potpourri, or an evergreen wreath or centerpiece. Gifts of food and favorite recipes also make wonderful presents. A bundle of recipe cards tied with a pretty ribbon, or a handmade book that contains 13 of your favorite recipes (one for each lunation) would also be very appreciated.

If you make a book, include several blank pages (or recipe cards) so that the recipient can add their own recipes, or perhaps journal about events that took place on the day they shared your recipe with others.

BROWN RICE YULE PORRIDGE

- 1 cup dry brown rice
- 2 cups water
- 1 cup unsweetened soy milk
- ⅓ cup brown sugar
- 1 tablespoon olive oil
- Sliced almonds and goji berries (optional)

Cook rice in water, covered over low heat for about 20 minutes or until done, stirring occasionally, until water has cooked off. Stir in soy milk, brown sugar, and olive oil. Mixture should be about same consistency as cooked oatmeal.

Serve topped with more brown sugar, agave, maple syrup, dried berries or fresh fruit, or your favorite nuts. Best is enjoyed immediately. Makes 2 to 3 servings.

2010
DECEMBER

SU	M	TU	W	TH	F	SA
			1	2	3	4
5 ● 12:36 pm	6	7	8	9	10	11
12	13	14	15	16	17	18
19	20	21 ☺ Long Nights Moon, 3:13 am Lunar Eclipse Yule/ Winter Solstice	22	23	24 Christmas Eve	25 Christmas Day
26	27	28	29	30	31 New Year's Eve	

When peace has been broken anywhere,
the peace of all countries everywhere is in danger.
~Franklin D. Roosevelt, SECOND INAUGURAL ADDRESS

Moon Void-of-Course

Last Aspect		New Sign	
Date	Time	Sign	NewTime

SEPTEMBER 2009

Date	Time	Sign	New Time
3	1:19 am	3 ♓	11:58 am
5	12:53 pm	5 ♈	10:14 am
7	8:12 pm	8 ♉	6:17 am
10	3:17 am	10 ♊	12:17 pm
12	7:30 am	12 ♋	4:19 pm
14	9:57 am	14 ♌	6:39 pm
16	12:10 pm	16 ♍	7:56 pm
18	7:56 pm	18 ♎	9:26 pm
20	2:43 pm	21 ♏	12:52 am
22	11:32 pm	23 ♐	7:43 am
25	10:15 am	25 ♑	6:19 pm
27	11:33 pm	28 ♒	7:06 am
30	7:34 am	30 ♓	7:26 pm

OCTOBER

Date	Time	Sign	New Time
2	11:29 pm	3 ♈	5:20 am
5	1:46 am	5 ♉	12:33 pm
7	1:19 pm	7 ♊	5:46 pm
9	9:35 pm	9 ♋	9:48 pm
11	9:37 pm	12 ♌	1:02 am
13	5:20 pm	14 ♍	3:45 am
16	6:18 am	16 ♎	6:29 am
18	1:33 am	18 ♏	10:22 am
20	2:57 pm	20 ♐	4:49 pm
23	1:13 am	23 ♑	2:39 am
25	2:14 pm	25 ♒	3:08 pm
28	3:22 am	28 ♓	3:45 am
30	12:56 am	30 ♈	1:56 pm

NOVEMBER

Date	Time	Sign	New Time
1	8:29 am	1 ♉	7:44 pm
3	1:04 pm	3 ♊	11:53 pm
5	10:47 pm	6 ♋	2:42 am
7	5:26 pm	8 ♌	5:23 am
9	9:43 pm	10 ♍	8:30 am
12	2:13 am	12 ♎	12:22 pm
14	6:10 am	14 ♏	5:24 pm
16	2:16 am	17 ♐	12:22 am
18	9:46 pm	19 ♑	10:00 am
21	10:04 pm	21 ♒	10:11 pm
23	10:35 pm	24 ♓	11:07 am
26	9:17 am	26 ♈	10:10 pm
28	6:32 pm	29 ♉	5:34 am

DECEMBER

Date	Time	Sign	New Time
1	8:39 am	1 ♊	9:23 am
3	5:27 am	3 ♋	11:00 am
5	12:08 am	5 ♌	12:07 pm
7	3:57 am	7 ♍	2:05 pm
9	5:04 am	9 ♎	5:47 pm
11	12:44 pm	11 ♏	11:31 pm
13	8:17 pm	14 ♐	7:25 am
16	7:02 am	16 ♑	5:32 pm
18	3:00 pm	19 ♒	5:38 am
21	7:53 am	21 ♓	6:42 pm
24	3:09 am	24 ♈	6:39 am
26	6:44 am	26 ♉	3:26 pm
28	12:54 pm	28 ♊	8:13 pm
30	3:29 pm	30 ♋	9:45 pm

JANUARY 2010

Date	Time	Sign	New Time
1	10:43 am	1 ♌	9:41 pm
3	4:55 pm	3 ♍	9:52 pm
5	12:25 pm	5 ♎	11:58 pm
8	1:07 am	8 ♏	5:00 am
10	10:02 am	10 ♐	1:10 pm
12	9:43 pm	12 ♑	11:54 pm
15	4:02 am	15 ♒	12:17 pm
17	3:22 pm	18 ♓	1:17 am
20	1:06 am	20 ♈	1:36 pm
22	2:46 pm	22 ♉	11:39 pm
24	10:03 pm	25 ♊	6:11 am
27	1:32 am	27 ♋	9:01 am
28	11:49 pm	29 ♌	9:10 am
31	1:27 am	31 ♍	8:23 am

FEBRUARY

Date	Time	Sign	New Time
1	11:17 am	2 ♎	8:42 am
4	4:27 am	4 ♏	11:56 am
6	11:11 am	6 ♐	7:04 pm
8	11:58 pm	9 ♑	5:43 am
11	7:39 am	11 ♒	6:24 pm
13	11:33 am	14 ♓	7:23 am
16	9:32 am	16 ♈	7:30 pm
18	10:52 pm	19 ♉	5:55 am
21	7:15 am	21 ♊	1:47 pm
23	12:29 pm	23 ♋	6:29 pm
25	12:48 pm	25 ♌	8:08 pm
27	3:15 pm	27 ♍	7:52 pm

MARCH

Date	Time	Sign	New Time
1	12:36 pm	1 ♎	7:31 pm
3	3:43 pm	3 ♏	9:11 pm
5	11:32 pm	6 ♐	2:36 am
8	6:13 am	8 ♑	12:13 pm
10	4:59 pm	11 ♒	12:42 am
13	7:57 am	13 ♓	1:44 pm
15	8:01 pm	16 ♈	2:32 am
18	7:23 am	18 ♉	12:29 pm
20	3:41 pm	20 ♊	8:28 pm
22	9:49 pm	23 ♋	2:16 am
25	12:39 am	25 ♌	5:39 am
27	3:04 am	27 ♍	6:57 am
29	2:55 am	29 ♎	7:21 am
31	8:13 am	31 ♏	8:41 am

APRIL

Date	Time	Sign	New Time
2	8:54 am	2 ♐	12:53 pm
4	4:57 pm	4 ♑	9:07 pm
7	4:18 am	7 ♒	8:51 am
9	5:44 pm	9 ♓	9:48 pm
12	8:51 am	12 ♈	9:31 am
14	3:23 pm	14 ♉	6:55 pm
17	12:57 am	17 ♊	2:08 am
19	6:21 am	19 ♋	7:39 am
21	10:07 am	21 ♌	11:42 am
23	11:35 am	23 ♍	2:24 pm
25	2:21 pm	25 ♎	4:16 pm
27	3:45 pm	27 ♏	6:28 pm
29	8:39 pm	29 ♐	10:36 pm

MAY

Date	Time	Sign	New Time
2	4:08 am	2 ♑	6:00 am
4	3:07 pm	4 ♒	4:52 pm
7	2:36 am	7 ♓	5:34 am
9	4:12 pm	9 ♈	5:29 pm
12	12:11 am	12 ♉	2:48 am
14	8:28 am	14 ♊	9:18 am
16	1:06 pm	16 ♋	1:46 pm
18	4:35 pm	18 ♌	5:06 pm
20	7:43 pm	20 ♍	7:58 pm
22	10:34 pm	22 ♎	10:50 pm
25	12:01 am	25 ♏	2:17 am
27	7:13 am	27 ♐	7:15 am
29	12:40 pm	29 ♑	2:44 pm
31	11:41 pm	6/1 ♒	1:08 am

JUNE

Date	Time	Sign	New Time
5/31	11:41 pm	1 ♒	1:08 am
3	10:56 am	3 ♓	1:34 pm
6	1:49 am	6 ♈	1:50 am
8	9:13 am	8 ♉	11:41 am
10	3:50 pm	10 ♊	6:11 pm
12	7:35 pm	12 ♋	9:50 pm
14	8:38 pm	14 ♌	11:54 pm
16	11:24 pm	17 ♍	1:41 am
19	1:04 am	19 ♎	4:13 am
21	5:44 am	21 ♏	8:14 am
23	11:32 am	23 ♐	2:10 pm
25	7:33 pm	25 ♑	10:21 pm
28	5:56 am	28 ♒	8:52 am
30	6:03 pm	30 ♓	9:10 am

JULY

Date	Time	Sign	New Time
3	7:17 am	3 ♈	9:44 am
5	5:24 pm	5 ♉	8:29 pm
8	2:10 am	8 ♊	5:49 am
10	6:17 am	10 ♋	7:38 am
12	7:48 am	12 ♌	8:53 am
14	6:23 am	14 ♍	7:01 pm
16	9:46 am	16 ♎	10:24 am
18	10:26 am	18 ♏	1:42 pm
20	7:43 am	20 ♐	7:58 pm
23	12:50 am	23 ♑	4:43 am
25	10:20 am	25 ♒	3:38 pm
27	11:46 pm	28 ♓	4:00 am
29	11:44 pm	30 ♈	4:42 pm

AUGUST

Date	Time	Sign	New Time
1	11:54 pm	2 ♉	4:13 am
4	8:44 am	4 ♊	12:54 pm
6	5:22 pm	6 ♋	5:50 pm
7	2:46 pm	8 ♌	7:23 pm
10	3:10 pm	10 ♍	7:01 pm
11	8:04 pm	12 ♎	6:43 pm
14	4:06 pm	14 ♏	8:26 pm
17	1:24 am	17 ♐	1:34 am
19	9:58 am	19 ♑	10:17 am
21	9:08 pm	21 ♒	9:37 pm
24	4:29 am	24 ♓	10:11 am